Fransjohan Pretorius

The Anglo-Boer War

1899–1902

STRUIK

Foreword

First published in 1985 by
Don Nelson

This edition published in 1998 by
Struik Publishers (Pty) Ltd
(a member of The Struik New Holland
Group of Companies)
Cornelis Struik House
80 McKenzie Street
Cape Town 8001

Reg. No.: 54/00965/07

Editor-in-chief: Professor D. J. van Zyl
Series editor: Lynne Bryer
Design: Poul-Ejnar Hansen
Cover Design: Dominic Robson
Picture research: Lynne Bryer
Photosetting: Diatype Setting
Lithographic reproduction:
Doble & Nagel
Printed and bound by CTP Book
Printers (Pty) Ltd

10 9 8 7 6 5 4 3 2 1

ISBN 1 86872 179 5

It is probably fitting that this work, which appeared in 1985 for the first time with Don Nelson Publishers, now sees a second revised edition on the threshold of the centenary of the Anglo-Boer War. I would therefore like to express the hope that you will enjoy it as a first acquaintance with that eventful period – officially a war between the Boers and the British, but in reality a struggle in which all groups in South Africa participated or which affected everyone in South Africa in some way or another – from there the name the South African War, which is used in academic circles.

A work of this scope obviously cannot do justice to each of the themes under discussion; an attempt has therefore been made to get to the heart of the matter without overburdening the reader with detail. Apart from the causes of the war and a survey of the military events, specific attention has been paid to themes from social and cultural history. Some of these have already been researched for purposes of advanced study. I gratefully acknowledge here the findings of other scholars in the field – research into Boer prisoners of war by Dr. S.P.R. Oosthuizen; Lords Roberts and Kitchener and civilians during the war by Professor S.B. Spies; Boer collaborators by Professor A.M. Grundlingh; and the position of blacks in the course of the conflict by Dr. P. Warwick. The work of Dr. G.D. Scholtz supplied useful insights into Europe's attitute to the war, while I personally had done some work on life on commando during the war.

I wish to thank Ms Linda de Villiers and Struik Publishers for this publication. I am also indebted to my parents and my wife, Laurette, who have experienced the Anglo-Boer War together with me for many years now, and my children, Laurette, Nicolaas and Hermann, who can point out with enthusiasm the most suitable places for blockhouses along the roads of South Africa.

FRANSJOHAN PRETORIUS
Pretoria, 1998

Contents

Maps

Every effort has been made to trace the owners of copyright for the quotations and illustrations used in this book. We apologise for any inadvertent oversight.

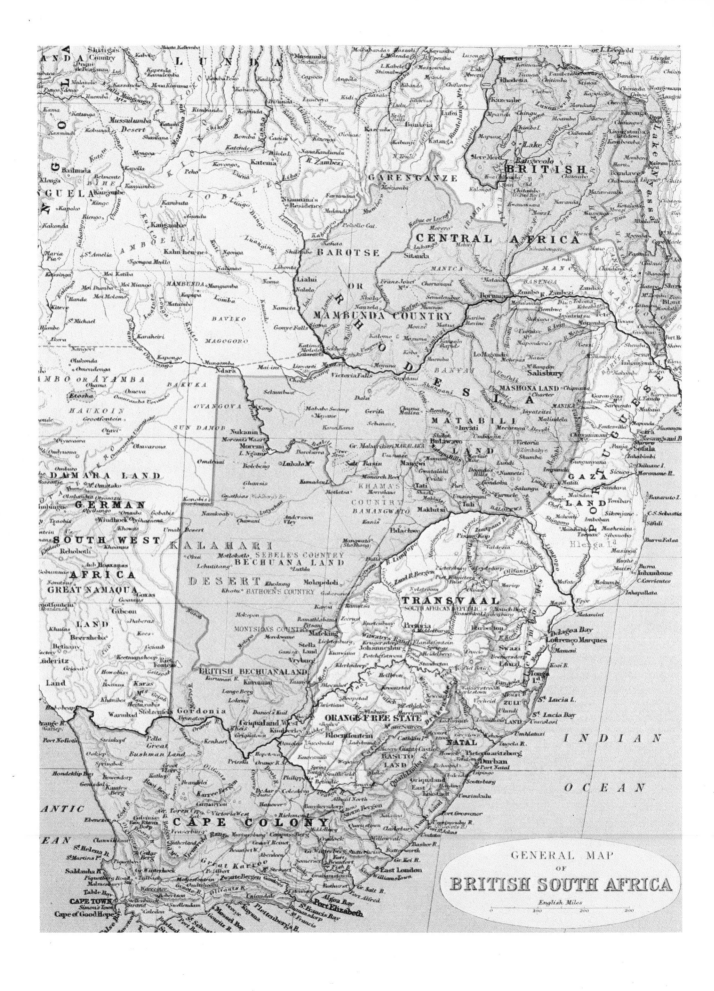

GENERAL MAP
OF
BRITISH SOUTH AFRICA

English Miles

CHAPTER 1

Prelude to the war

In the last years of the 19th century British imperialism and Afrikaner nationalism met in a conflict that culminated in the Anglo-Boer War of 1899-1902. British imperialists were convinced that the leaders of Afrikaner nationalism posed a threat to imperial interests in South Africa, while the advocates of Afrikaner nationalism feared that British imperialists were intent on destroying Afrikaner independence. On both sides the conviction grew that there was not enough room for the two ideologies to coexist in South Africa, and each developed a suspicion of the other so deep that it bedevilled any possible diplomatic solution.

At the time the Cape and Natal were British colonies, while to the north of the Orange River were two independent Boer republics: the Orange Free State between the Orange and the Vaal, and the Zuid-Afrikaansche Republiek (the Transvaal).

The concept of a federation of South African states, proposed at the time by British Colonial Secretary Lord Carnarvon, led to the annexation of the Zuid-Afrikaansche Republiek on 12 April 1877. For the Afrikaners the loss of their independence was unbearable. In reaction to British expansionism under the banner of

Left The theatre of war, showing how the Boer republics were all but encircled by British territory (*Transvaal War*)

Right The Jameson Raid was a crucial forerunner of the war. French pro-Boer reaction is revealed in this cover picture from *Le Petit Journal,* January 1896

7

imperialism, a spirit of nationalism was awakened among Afrikaners far beyond the borders of the Transvaal. In the Cape Colony the Afrikaner Bond was founded in 1879 and soon branches flourished also in the Orange Free State and Transvaal.

After the annexation Transvalers initially adopted a policy of passive resistance. Only after two fruitless visits by Paul Kruger to London (where the Imperial government made its determination to uphold the annexation clear) did the Transvaal burghers turn to armed resistance in December 1880. This ended in victory for the Transvaal 'Boers' at the Battle of Majuba on 27 February 1881.

The Pretoria Convention of 3 August 1881 did not fully reinstate the independence of the ZAR, but kept the republic under British suzerainty. This vague concept basically meant that Britain retained supervisory control of the foreign affairs of the ZAR and of its internal legislation with regard to blacks.

The London Convention of 27 February 1884 conferred full internal independence on the ZAR, but whether this relieved the ZAR of British suzerainty was not regarded as an immediate issue. The ZAR government, however, accepted that this was indeed the case, as did British Prime Minister William Gladstone. More than 12 years later the issue would be raised once more by the British. Article IV of the London Convention stipulated that the ZAR would not be allowed to conclude any agreements with any state or nation other than the Orange Free State, or with any black tribe to the east or west of the ZAR without the approval of Great Britain.

The discovery of gold on the Witwatersrand in 1886 initiated a new phase in relations between British imperialists and Afrikaner nationalists. The thousands of Uitlanders, as the immigrants who rushed to the goldfields to seek their fortune were called, were mostly British subjects. Fearing that the Uitlanders would threaten the independence of the ZAR, the Volksraad in 1890 increased the period of residence required for enfranchisement and nationalisation from five to 14 years. While most of the Uitlanders had no intention of surrendering their British citizenship, some of the mining magnates began demanding a voice in the government of the ZAR.

At the height of tension between President Kruger and members of the Uitlander community, Cecil John Rhodes, then Prime Minister of the Cape Colony, came to the aid of the Uitlanders. As a dedicated imperialist, Rhodes wished to see all of

South Africa united under the British flag and was engaged in a policy of encircling the ZAR with British territory. By the middle of the 1890s the ZAR was hedged in on the western, northern and south-eastern side with British territories. The republic's only remaining non-British contact with the outside world was through Delagoa Bay in Portuguese East Africa (Moçambique). Rhodes tried in vain to buy the port from the Portuguese. To his intense frustration, the ZAR escaped land-locked isolation when its railway line between Pretoria and Delagoa Bay was at last completed in 1894, affording the ZAR greater economic independence from the British colonies in South Africa. In a final effort to bring the ZAR under British control, Rhodes took a lead in organising the Jameson Raid. The Reform Committee, consisting of prominent Uitlanders, was to start a rising in Johannesburg while Rhodes's protegé, Dr Leander Starr Jameson, was to rush to their aid from Bechuanaland with an armed force and overthrow the ZAR government.

The Jameson Raid took place around New Year, 1896. It was poorly planned and General Piet Cronjé of the ZAR forced the invaders to surrender before they could reach Johannesburg. Wisely, President Kruger showed lenience towards the invaders and Uitlanders involved in the plot, as well as making certain concessions to the Uitlanders in general. But the rift between the ZAR government and the Uitlanders deepened. Relations worsened between the republic and Britain, where a new Unionist (Conservative) Party had come into power under Prime Minister Lord Salisbury in June 1895. The ZAR government mistrusted the motives of the British, particularly those of Colonial Secretary Joseph Chamberlain. Suspicion was deepened by the Boer belief that British government officials in South Africa, as well as Chamberlain himself, had been involved in Rhodes's attempted coup d'etat.

Historians today agree that Chamberlain had been fully aware of Rhodes's plot and had actively supported it by granting Jameson's British South Africa Company land in the Bechuanaland Protectorate, from where the invasion was launched.

Opposite A top-hatted President Kruger inspects the Transvaal State Artillery leaving for the front (*De Vrijheids-Oorlog*)

Above Cecil Rhodes, photographed during the siege of Kimberley in the white trousers he wore informally. His dream of British control over South Africa was realised by the war – but at enormous cost, and two months after his death (Dennis Edwards)

Moreover, a South Africa united under the British flag was an ideal cherished by Chamberlain, who intended controlling Rhodes to the point where Britain, and not the Cape Colony, would eventually be in control of Southern Africa. The two Boer republics were aware of this intention, which hardened their resistance to unification under the British flag. The resultant resurgence of nationalism brought Afrikaners throughout South Africa closer together. The Cape Afrikaners identified themselves anew with the Afrikaners of the Boer republics. The Afrikaner Bond broke with Rhodes, who was forced to resign as Prime Minister after the Jameson Raid. The Free State, which regarded the raid as an attack on its own independence, reaffirmed and strengthened its 1889 political alliance with the ZAR in March 1897. In terms of this agreement, the Boer republics would come to each other's assistance should the independence of either be threatened. After the Jameson Raid the republics began buying large quantities of arms and ammunition from Germany and France in order to prepare for a possible future onslaught.

The Jameson Raid and Afrikaner reaction to it caused those South African British who had imperialist sympathies to unite in the South African League. The League's aim was to maintain British supremacy in South Africa and to secure equal political rights for all whites in a South Africa united under the British flag. South Africans were now divided into two

9

'Troops embarking for South Africa', from a British postcard. Britain dispatched an expeditionary force of 47 000 between October and December 1899, to join the 10 000 troops already stationed in South Africa. Another 5 600 were sent from regiments in India (Greenwall collection)

camps, with the British camp the more powerful precisely because the initiative would largely be taken in Britain itself.

Britain's interest in the ZAR, and in a South Africa united under her flag, stemmed chiefly from important strategic and economic considerations. In the surge of neo-imperialism after 1870 the scramble for Africa became a race for colonies between Britain, France, Belgium and Italy, and later Germany also. In the subsequent partition of Africa, Britain regarded the entire subcontinent, including the ZAR, as her sphere of influence. Control of the Cape Colony was important for the protection of the sea route to Britain's valuable possessions in the East. However, control of the Southern African interior – including the ZAR, with its connection to a port on the east coast – would safeguard the sea route further, a consideration all the more pressing since Germany had annexed German South West Africa and German East Africa in 1884, thereby intruding on Britain's sphere of influence in the subcontinent. When Kaiser Wilhelm

II sent Kruger a telegram of congratulations after the abortive Jameson Raid, Britain's concern over Germany's sympathy and her possible aid to the ZAR deepened.

British interest in the ZAR had now gained a political motive in addition to strategic and economic considerations. On 30 August 1898 Britain concluded an agreement with Germany, her colonial competitor, to render joint financial aid to a weakened Portugal; in this way Britain acquired certain rights in some of the Portuguese colonies. Delagoa Bay was to be drawn into the British sphere of influence, which in effect meant that Germany was leaving the ZAR to the mercy of Britain. In acquiring control over the ZAR, Britain would reaffirm her position as a leading world power.

This political motive had its spiritual origin in British national pride. Charles Darwin had pointed out the theory of the survival of the fittest in his *The Origin of Species* (1859); a similar so-called social Darwinism regarding the behaviour of man came to the fore: in the struggle for existence the strongest triumphed, while the weak succumbed. The concept served to strengthen nationalism and patriotism – the love of one's own – and awakened the desire for expansion or

imperialism. British 'race patriotism' ran high. Joseph Chamberlain, one of the foremost champions of imperialism, believed that British culture surpassed all others. To bring the ZAR under British cultural influence would be 'good for the Boers'. British imperialism, at bottom, was a form of aggressive nationalism.

The discovery of gold has often been pinpointed as the major cause of the Anglo-Boer War, particularly when deep-level mining revealed the immense wealth of the Witwatersrand mines in the mid 1890s. This allegedly stimulated British desire to acquire the ZAR. But this is a somewhat simplistic view. In truer perspective, by 1895 deep-level mining had transferred the economic focus of Southern Africa from the Cape Colony to the ZAR; as a result, the ZAR posed a threat to British supremacy in South Africa. This was reason enough for seeking to bring the Republic under British control.

Chamberlain consequently evinced an imperialistic interest in the grievances of the Uitlanders, whom he planned to use as tools in his onslaught on the ZAR. His strategy was twofold: by intervention in the internal affairs of the ZAR he planned to force humiliating capitulations on the Republic, and secondly he planned to claim that the ZAR was subordinate to Britain.

The London Convention provided Chamberlain with the weapon he needed. In terms of Article IV, the ZAR required Britain's approval of all treaties with other states, with the exception of the Orange Free State. Chamberlain alleged that the ZAR was subordinate to Britain and that the suzerainty of the Pretoria Convention had not been negated by the London Convention. Though Chamberlain was probably mistaken in this, the interpretation afforded him grounds for protesting against three laws of the ZAR in 1896: the Aliens Expulsion Law, the Immigration Law, and the Press Law, all aimed at curbing the influence of the Uitlanders.

In May 1897 Chamberlain appointed Sir Alfred Milner High Commissioner for South Africa, a move which proved a turning point in Anglo-British relations. Milner's brilliant administrative career in Egypt and as

Left Queen Victoria listens to a dispatch from the front. Britain had not foreseen the magnitude of her losses (*Transvaal War*)

Above British mounted infantry, painted in 1901 by Dutch artist Frans Oerder, who had joined the Boer forces in 1899 (Greenwall collection)

Below 'Grandmother goes to war' a humorous Belgian postcard (Greenwall collection)

chairman of the Board of Inland Revenue in London had equipped him well for his task in South Africa; in him, Chamberlain found an imperialist ally as fervent as himself. The inflexible Milner, who regarded himself as a 'British race patriot' was, like Chamberlain, a protagonist of a federation of South African states under the British flag. He saw it as his task to protect this section of the British Empire against the danger of Afrikaner nationalism. As the focus of Afrikaner nationalism, the ZAR was to be destroyed so that all South Africa might be included in the British Empire.

How well founded was Milner's fear that Afrikaner nationalism posed a threat to British supremacy in South Africa? Most of the Afrikaner leaders were not in favour of the idea of a united South Africa. Though Kruger was prepared to allow closer association between the ZAR and other South African states up to the point when the independence of the ZAR appeared threatened, he nevertheless refused to view the issue from a broader South African perspective. Protagonists of Afrikaner nationalism were unable to ignore the fact that all Afrikaners were now obliged to take a stand, either as republicans or as monarchists. The leaders of the ZAR appear to have realised that for this very reason they could expect no more than moral support from the Cape members of the Afrikaner Bond. The limitations imposed by the London Convention made even the Free State cautious of an alliance with the ZAR; a loose federal union in which both republics would retain their independence was as much as could be envisaged.

Milner did not subscribe to this view. His initial patience soon yielded to action when the equally inflexible Kruger was re-elected President of the ZAR by an overwhelming majority in February 1898. On 23 February 1898 Milner wrote to Chamberlain: 'There is no way out of the political troubles of South Africa except reform in the Transvaal or war.' From this point on, Milner's diplomatic strategy was aimed at provoking a serious quarrel with the ZAR over the Uitlander question; their grievances would provide a pretext for British intervention. Milner also co-operated with Chamberlain in preparing the press and the public in Britain for the

UNE PROMENADE.

Grand'maman va-t-en guerre.

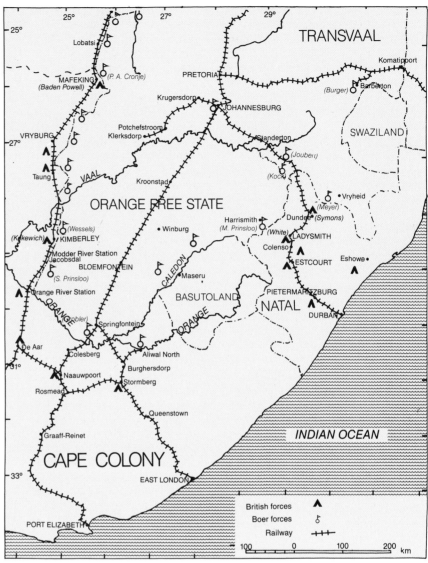

Above Map showing the disposition of major Boer and British forces at the outbreak of war

Top left Sir Alfred (later Lord) Milner, British High Commissioner in South Africa, was one of the prime movers behind the drift towards war (*War with the Boers*)

Left Though President Marthinus Steyn of the Orange Free State had done all he could to prevent war, he did not fail to call out his burghers in support of Kruger (Cape Archives)

possibility of war should a satisfactory solution not be found to Uitlander grievances.

The gravity of the Uitlander case was probably overestimated. Uitlander men may well have slightly outnumbered Transvaal burghers in the ZAR but Kruger, like everyone else, mistakenly estimated that the Uitlanders were far and away in the majority. He had extended the period of residence required for enfranchisement from five to 14 years to prevent them from taking over the ZAR government. However, it is clear that the average Uitlander was not interested in either naturalisation or the vote. The true grievances may be traced to the magnates and the mining companies. With good reason, they argued that Kruger's industrial policy considerably increased the costs of mining, particularly when industrial concessions and monopolies were awarded to the privileged, precluding free enterprise and competition in the open market. Concessions for liquor, dynamite and rail transport were a source of great discord between the Chamber of Mines and the ZAR government. Rejection of the Industrial Commission's recommendations in 1897 further stressed the inflexibility of the ZAR government. It was accused of corruption, and it cannot be disputed that its civil service was sorely in need of a thorough revision.

During Milner's visit to London towards the end of 1898, tension mounted in the ZAR. In December a British subject, Tom Edgar, was shot by a Constable Jones in the course of duty. The Uitlanders' South African League seized the opportunity to incite opposition to the government.

Milner returned to South Africa in early 1899 after smoothing the way for action against the ZAR. From this time on the diplomatic initiative undoubtedly rested with him; Chamberlain and the British Cabinet merely reacted to Milner's moves. By misrepresenting the situation in South Africa, he prepared the Cabinet and British public for war as a solution to the 'Transvaal problem' and succeeded in magnifying the internal dispute between Kruger and the Uitlanders into an international issue.

This was made particularly clear when with Milner's encouragement an Uitlander petition containing close on 22 000 signatures was sent direct to Queen Victoria in March 1899. The petition voiced Uitlander grievances, urging voting rights and British intervention. To back up the petition, Milner telegraphed his famous 'Helot's Despatch' of 4 May 1899 to Chamberlain, concluding that there was more than enough reason for intervention in the ZAR where, he alleged, thousands of British subjects were permanently placed in the position of helots or slaves. Britain's influence and prestige were, he claimed, being seriously undermined.

President M. T. Steyn of the Free State and W. P. Schreiner, Prime Minister of the Cape Colony, both tried to prevent the impending war. Steyn invited Milner and Kruger to a conference in Bloemfontein, where they met on 31 May 1899 for talks that lasted until 5 June. Kruger was prepared to give the Uitlanders the vote after seven years' residence, but the demands he made in return for this concession endangered the success of the conference. He demanded for instance the incorporation of Swaziland into the ZAR, compensation for the Jameson Raid and arbitration over the London Convention. Milner refused to concede to these demands, insisting on only five years' residence as a qualification for the vote. When Kruger refused, Milner broke off negotiations.

The failure of the conference heralded the last stage of the crisis preceding the war. Milner returned from Bloemfontein convinced that war was the only remaining solution if Britain were to retain her position as ruling power in South Africa. He therefore asked the British government to increase the garrison in South Africa immediately by 10 000 troops. Further negotiations between Britain and the ZAR over the Uitlander vote failed dismally. After Bloemfontein Boer leaders were convinced that Milner and Chamberlain were not to be trusted. To them, too, war seemed to be the only solution. So the tension mounted.

Britain was in a position of immense strength. Supreme at sea, she could if necessary cut off the ZAR's foreign supplies. With the whole of the Empire behind her, she could muster enormous numbers of troops, limitless resources and vast supplies of food and munitions. On 8 September 1899, the British government shipped 10 000 troops to South Africa, bringing the total of troops on the republican borders to 22 000. Fourteen days later the British government decided on war and drafted an ultimatum to the ZAR, holding it back until the British troops were in position.

The ZAR and its ally, the Orange Free State, watched the concentration of troops on their borders with growing alarm. On 27 September Commandant-General Piet Joubert called up between 56 and 65 per cent of the Transvaal commandos and ordered them to the borders. Six days later Steyn gave Free State burghers the same order. Though he had tried to prevent the war, he was determined to honour his agreement of March 1897.

The ZAR played into Britain's hands by issuing an ultimatum on 9 October 1899. It demanded that all 'points of mutual difference' between Britain and the ZAR be settled by arbitration, that the British troops 'on the borders of this Republic . . . be instantly withdrawn', and that troops en route to South Africa by sea should not be landed at any South African port. Britain was given 48 hours to comply. If she failed to accept these terms, the ZAR would 'with great regret be compelled to regard the action as a formal declaration of war'.

'They have done it!' exclaimed Chamberlain, for with this ultimatum the Kruger regime had become the aggressor. British public opinion was stirred, ensuring loyal participation in the war effort. Consequently Britain refused the ultimatum. At 17h00 on 11 October 1899 the Second Anglo-Boer War broke out.

A Boer commando rides out of Pretoria for the front. (War with the Boers)

CHAPTER 2

Military operations

The Boer offensive

With the outbreak of hostilities on 11 October 1899 the bulk of the British troops had not yet arrived in South Africa, giving the Boer forces the opportunity of taking the initiative in the offensive. The primary objective of the Boer command was to isolate or wipe out the British forces threatening the republics on their borders. Their secondary aim was to occupy suitable positions in enemy territory where the Boer forces could halt the advance of British reinforcements moving up from the coast.

The largest concentration of British troops at this stage was on the Natal front in the east. Lieutenant-General Sir George White had 9 600 men at Ladysmith, while Major-General Sir W. Penn Symons and 5 000 troops were stationed at Dundee. On the Boer side, Commandant-General Piet Joubert had mustered 11 400 Transvalers and 6 000 Free Staters at various points on the Natal front. Joubert's primary objective was to crush the British force at Dundee and proceed to Ladysmith, the junction of the railway line between the Free State, Transvaal and Natal.

In the first battle waged in Natal – the Battle of Talana or Dundee, on 20 October 1899 – General Lucas Meyer failed in his objective and the enemy were allowed to escape to Ladysmith with their mortally wounded commander Penn Symons. Boer losses were fewer than 150, while some 500 British soldiers had been put out of action. On the following day, 21 October, the Boer offensive against White's garrison at Elandslaagte was repulsed by the British at the Battle of Elandslaagte. British cavalry killed some of the fleeing Boers in a particularly gruesome manner with their lances. Boer losses, chiefly amongst the Hollander Volunteer Corps, were 336 men, of whom 46 died. The Boer Commander, General J.H.M. Kock, was fatally wounded. British casualties numbered 263, of whom 50 died.

'Mournful Monday', as 30 October 1899 was called, cost the British 1 764 casualties when White failed to scatter the Transvaal and Orange Free State commandos at Modderspruit and Nicholson's Nek. With White's troops isolated at Ladysmith, Joubert and 2 000 burghers undertook a reconnaissance as far as Estcourt in Natal. Their objective was to find defensible positions with a view to blocking the march of British reinforcements from the coast. Near Chieveley a commando under General Louis Botha captured an armoured train on 15 November; amongst the passengers taken prisoner was Winston Churchill, war correspondent for the *Morning Post*. A few weeks later he escaped from Pretoria and rejoined the British forces.

After long delays, Joubert's expedition fell back to Colenso in late November, taking up a position on the northern bank of the Tugela River. Here Joubert prepared to resist the large British force marching from southern Natal; several battalions

had arrived from overseas and were concentrated around Estcourt and Mooi River. Joubert suffered serious injury when his horse stumbled, so that from 30 November leadership at the Tugela passed to the energetic and brilliant Louis Botha, then 37 years old.

On the western front the Boers took the lead in the offensive but lost valuable time by their tardiness. General Piet Cronjé and his 6 000 burghers had been delegated to isolate and crush the British troops on the western front. A weak British force of some 1 000 whites, plus 300 armed blacks acting as herdsmen, were stationed at Mafeking (Mafikeng) under Colonel Robert Baden-Powell. On 13 October 1899 Mafeking was completely encircled by Boer forces after General Koos de la Rey's capture of an armoured train at Kraaipan the evening before, in the first action of the war. By 3 November some 4 800 Free State burghers under Chief Commandant C. J. Wessels and 2 200

Transvaal burghers under de la Rey had completely besieged Lieutenant-Colonel R. G. Kekewich and his force of 2 600 men at Kimberley.

Much criticism has been levelled at Joubert and Cronjé for concentrating several thousand burghers in a senseless siege that lasted several months. The burghers might have been deployed elsewhere, or might have struck deeper into enemy territory without delay, to prevent British reinforcement and cut off their supply of ammunition. But the long series of major battles waged by General Sir Redvers Buller in Natal, and by Lieutenant-General Lord Methuen on the western front, to relieve the sieges of Ladysmith, Kimberley and Mafeking, did result in serious losses on the British side. Nevertheless the sieges retarded the Boer offensive, and when their reinforcements landed, the British were able to take the lead in the offensive.

On the southern and south-western front, Boer military leaders made sev-

Above Repeated brave attempts were made by the British to save 12 field guns stranded during the battle of Colenso on 15 December 1899. Colonel Long had blundered in advancing his gun teams ahead of the infantry battalions, so that they came under heavy fire from the Mausers of the Krugersdorp commando under Sarel Oosthuizen, concealed in trenches beyond the Tugela River. This dramatic watercolour of the rescue attempt during which Lord Roberts' son Freddy was mortally wounded, was painted by Sidney Paget, illustrator for *The Sphere* (Greenwall collection)

Inset, chapter head Local colonial troops played an important role in the Anglo-Boer War, not least because of their knowledge of terrain and conditions. Watercolour by T. Gilson of a South African mounted trooper (Greenwall collection)

Opposite S. E. St Leger of the Royal Irish Regiment captured some of the calm stoicism of the Boer soldier in his portrait of 'A Transvaal burgher'. Watercolour original for St Leger's book *War Sketches in Colour* (Greenwall collection)

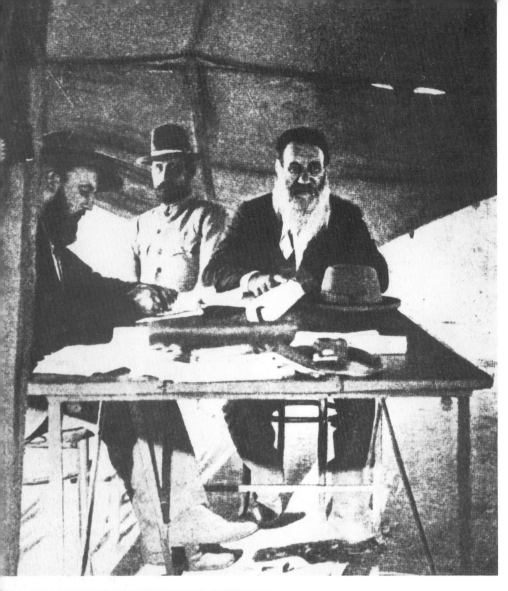

eral mistakes. They mustered only 3 200 burghers and of the three strategic railway junctions – Stormberg, Naauwpoort and De Aar – they occupied only the first.

It was the middle of November 1899 before Chief-Commandant J. H. Olivier succeeded in forcing the British troops in the Stormberg to fall back to Queenstown. The fact that commandos under General H. Schoeman penetrated only as far as Colesberg, and failed to occupy the railway junctions at Naauwpoort and De Aar immediately, further contributed to the collapse of the Boer offensive. With the railways in British hands, the Boers found themselves unable to halt the British advance through the Cape.

On the northern front the small number of British troops in Rhodesia (Zimbabwe) were kept in check by a

Boer force of some 2 000 under General F. A. Grobler. When a month passed without Grobler taking the offensive, the campaign was abandoned.

The first British offensive fails

While the Boer forces advanced sluggishly at the outbreak of the war, British reinforcements continued to arrive in South Africa. British campaign strategy had originally intended General Sir Redvers Buller, as Commander-in-Chief of the British forces in South Africa, to march via the Cape Colony along the railway line (which would provide him with vital provisions) and conquer the Boer republics from the south. However, White's inability to defend Natal drastically altered the situation. On his arrival in Cape Town on 31 October 1899, Buller therefore decided rather to relieve Ladysmith and Kimberley as soon as possible and halt the Boer offensive in Natal and the northern Cape. With this aim, Methuen was to march along the western railway line to relieve Kimberley. Major-General J. P. D. French at Colesberg and Lieutenant-General Sir William Gatacre near Stormberg were to repulse the Boer invasion of the Cape Colony. Buller would himself undertake the task of recapturing northern Natal and relieving Ladysmith. The first British offensive swung into motion.

Buller arrived in Natal on 25 November 1899. His reinforcements joined him at Frere, so that two weeks later his troops numbered more than 21 000, with 46 guns. In the hills along the Tugela north of Colenso Louis Botha and his 4 500 Transvaal Boers and five guns blocked the way of the British to Ladysmith. Higher up along the upper Tugela a force of 2 000 Free State Boers lay in wait. Botha had his burghers dig trenches and build outworks of rock and sandbags in front of the hills near the river. Eventually 3 000 burghers were to take part in the Battle of Colenso on 15 December 1899.

Unimaginatively, Buller decided on a frontal attack on the Boer positions. Hopelessly inadequate reconnaissance had failed to determine the positions of the Boer entrenchments in front of the hills. Fatally, he also failed to correct the mistakes on his maps. On the morning of 15 December, warned by two days' continuous bombardment of the hills behind them, the Boers in their concealed positions unleashed a hail of rifle and cannon fire on the enemy advancing across the Tugela. Buller's forces suffered a disastrous defeat. Boer losses totalled 38, but Buller had lost at least 1 139 men.

When his first attempt to relieve Ladysmith ended in dismal failure, Buller heliographed a message to White in Ladysmith advising that if he could not last out another month, he was to shoot away as much ammunition as possible and accept the most favourable terms. This message has contributed much to the criticism levelled at Buller over the years.

In an attempt to relieve the boredom of their burghers and occupy Ladysmith, General Schalk Burger and Chief Commandant Marthinus Prinsloo launched an attack on Platrand, south of Ladysmith, on the morning of 6 January 1900. Lack of sound leadership and co-operation on the Boer side, and the courageous defence put up by the British, caused the failure of this Boer offensive.

Buller's defeat at Colenso led to his replacement by Field-Marshall Lord Roberts as supreme commander of the British forces in South Africa. Before Roberts' arrival in South Africa, Buller made a second attempt to break through to Ladysmith. With reinforcements, his force numbered some 30 000 men by 23 January 1900. He decided to cross the Tugela a few kilometres west of Colenso and encircle the Boers' right flank.

Though the violent encounter of 24 January 1900 represented the climax, the Battle of Spionkop had in fact begun on 16 January with British troops crossing the Tugela under Lieutenant-General Sir Charles Warren. His mission was to take Spionkop in order to be in a position to threaten the Boers on Tabanyama Hill. There on Spionkop the British column of 2 000 men under Major-General E. R. P. Woodgate was pinned down by the Boers on the morning of 24 January. Some 400 burghers under Commandant Hendrik Prinsloo of Carolina and Commandant 'Rooi Daniel' Opperman of Pretoria district stormed up Spionkop and opened fire on the British with deadly accuracy. From the hills rising in a crescent around Spionkop, rifles and guns spewed destruction. In the biggest battle of the war the British suffered their most serious reverse. It lasted nine days, and the toll on the British side was 2 500 to 2 700 casualties, of which between 1 800 and 2 000 occurred on 24 January alone. Boer losses totalled less than 200.

A third attempt to relieve Ladysmith collapsed at Vaalkrans, a hill between Colenso and Spionkop, from 5 to 7 February 1900. Buller's failure must be attributed to his poor intelligence regarding Boer positions across the Tugela, as well as to the courage of the Johannesburg Commando and the Boer artillery.

Above Louis Botha, a man with an imposing physical presence, assumed command during Joubert's illness before Colenso (*L'Illustration*)

Opposite top left General Piet Joubert with his son-in-law and secretary in his tent outside Ladysmith (*Heroes*)

Top right Lord Roberts arrived in Cape Town on 10 January 1900 as supreme commander of the British forces in South Africa (*Die Buren*)

Opposite below Winston Churchill, war correspondent, arrives in Durban from Lourenço Marques after his escape from Boer capture (Greenwall collection)

Overleaf 'Night Patrol, Modder River 1899' – Seaforth Highlanders before the major battle of Magersfontein, where they would suffer such devastating losses. Watercolour by Private J. Farquharson (Greenwall collection)

In the meantime, Methuen on the western front had received orders from Buller to push through to Kimberley as fast as possible. With a force of 10 500 men and successive reinforcements, he succeeded in driving some 3 600 Boers from their positions at Belmont and Graspan on 23 and 25 November.

At Graspan (also called Enslin or Rooilaagte), de la Rey and Buller came face to face for the first time. On 28 November they again clashed at Modder River (Tweeriviere). De la Rey's experiences at Graspan had taught him that hills were not the ideal position they had formerly been considered to be. The wide view from the hills did not compensate for the accurate artillery fire the Boers had to endure there. De la Rey therefore convinced his fellow officers that the steep banks at the confluence of the Modder and Riet Rivers would offer them the best defence against Methuen's approaching force.

The unsuspecting British troops – the result of Methuen's poor reconnaissance – walked straight into the Boer positions. Though the burghers opened fire prematurely, their bullets caused havoc amongst the British in a battle that raged until sundown.

The Boers were however once again forced to fall back when the Free Staters on the western flank under Combat-General J. Prinsloo left

their key positions, exposing the other burghers to danger. The Boers then stationed themselves at the Magersfontein kopjes bisecting the railway line. De la Rey's experience had convinced him that the kopjes themselves were not the best line of defence, but rather the plain at the foot of the hills. Anticipating that Methuen would direct his attack at the hills, de la Rey had his burghers dig themselves into a concealed line of trenches in front of and parallel to the ridges. In contrast to the broad, shallow trenches of the British, the Boer trenches were straight-sided and about a metre deep and a metre wide. The Boers could stand upright in them and shoot over breastworks of soil almost totally camouflaged by branches and grass.

De la Rey's trenches at Magersfontein were not the first in modern warfare: trenches had been used as early as the Crimean War of 1854-56 and the American Civil War of 1860-64. Nevertheless de la Rey's unusual decision to position his trenches on the plains in front of the hills marked him as a superior strategist.

On the afternoon of 10 December 1899, Methuen opened artillery fire in earnest on the ridges of Magersfontein. He had no inkling of the actual positions of the Boers, and de la Rey's camouflaged trenches formed a perfect trap. Ironically de la Rey himself

was not present at the Battle of Magersfontein. He had left a few days earlier to recuperate north of Kimberley from a shoulder wound. Piet Cronjé was in command of the 8 000 Boers with their 10 guns; against them Methuen had mustered 33 guns and 15 000 men.

Early on the morning of 11 December the unsuspecting British troops, with the Highland Brigade in the vanguard, ran into the deadly fire from the Boer trenches. The British advanced in closed formation, thereby suffering enormous losses from the outset. Methuen did not recover from this initial reverse. With shock he watched as the Boers not only halted the Highland Brigade in front of Magersfontein Kop but also his cavalry southeast of the Kop. By twilight, when the guns fell silent, the Boers had suffered 255 casualties. It is generally accepted that the British casualties were considerably higher than the 971 given by the *Times History*.

De la Rey was disappointed in Cronjé's decision not to pursue the British immediately and annihilate them. Despite Boer failure to press home their advantage, the first British offensive on the western front had proved a humiliating failure.

On the southern front many Cape colonists who sympathised with the Boer cause had joined the Boer forces. In an attempt to quell this rebellious mood and restore British prestige, Gatacre decided to repel the Boer force of 1 000 men and two guns at Stormberg with 20 guns and over 5 000 men. Without any reconnaissance Gatacre set out on an exhausting night march, lost his way, and, on the morning of 10 December 1899, ran into the Boer force led by Chief Commandant J. H. Olivier. The deadly accuracy of the Boer rifle fire decided the battle. Between 700 and 800 British soldiers were put out of action, while the Boer casualties were 21 men.

The British reverses at Stormberg, Magersfontein and Colenso on 10, 11 and 15 December 1899 respectively became known as 'Black Week' in Britain. The British reeled at the realisation that a handful of farmers were teaching their mighty empire a lesson in warfare. The first British offensive had failed for the same reason as the Boer attack, as the result of poor leadership. Buller, Methuen and Gatacre were unequal to this type of warfare, though Methuen was ultimately to emerge from the war with his honour restored. By their frontal attacks and inadequate intelligence, the British generals had played into the hands of the Boers, concealed behind their well-camouflaged entrenchments.

The failure of the first British offensive was not exploited by the Boer leaders. Their victories had placed the Boers in a position to resume the initiative, to encircle the enemy, particularly in the Cape Colony, and to destroy the railway lines behind Methuen and Gatacre. Presidents Kruger and Steyn had urged these moves upon Cronjé; and Generals de la Rey and Christiaan de Wet were prepared to take on the campaign with 1 500 burghers. But Cronjé refused to weaken his force to this extent, failing to realise that the Boers could have taken the important railway junctions at De Aar and even Naauwpoort – a manoeuvre that would have seriously hampered Roberts' advance to the Free State.

The second British offensive succeeds

On 10 January 1900, Field Marshal Lord Roberts arrived in South Africa to assume supreme command of the British forces. Lord Kitchener accompanied him as Chief of Staff. Roberts decided to conquer the Boer republics from the Cape Colony, in keeping with original British strategy. However, he regarded the western railway line as the most suitable route for his advance, and the relief of Kimberley as his first objective. Thereafter he had to abandon the railway line in an eastward attack on Bloemfontein, and finally march on Pretoria.

Roberts replaced Buller and Methuen's tactics of frontal attack with those of encirclement. This would give him the opportunity of attacking the Boers from the rear. For this purpose cavalry was important; high priority was given to mobility. A new division of cavalry was organised under General Sir John French and more mounted infantrymen pushed into the field.

The British reverses of December had stressed the need for a dramatic increase of British troops in South Africa. Roberts alone was to have a force of some 50 000 troops at his disposal for the forthcoming campaign, a figure that did not include Buller's force on the Natal front.

By mobilising a large sector of his forces at Colesberg in the south, Roberts detracted the attention of the Boer military leaders – all except Cronjé – from his true target in the west. The British force at Colesberg engaged the attention of the Boers to such an extent that they neglected the defence of the western front. From Magersfontein, where he had entrenched himself after the battle, Cronjé warned his fellow-officers repeatedly but in vain.

In order to relieve Kimberley, Roberts held the attention of Cronjé and de Wet with an infantry division, while French's mounted division moved off in a wide arc through the Free State to the east of Jacobsdal, past Cronjé's left flank. After a forced march, French rode into Kimberley on 15 February 1900 – a military coup that confirmed Roberts' abilities as a tactician. However, it should be borne in mind that he had at his disposal a far larger force, with more artillery than Methuen and Buller had commanded in their failed campaigns.

Further back at Magersfontein, Cronjé was taken completely by sur-

General Koos de la Rey (*above*) ensured his place in history by his use of trenches at Magersfontein. Though trenches were not new in warfare, de la Rey's use of them was inspired. Strategically placed just in front of the line of hills, they provided perfect camouflage for the Boers (Postcard, Greenwall collection)

The actual photograph of the trenches shows how unobtrusive they were, while the two cross-section drawings illustrate how well the trenches were improved after the battle of Magersfontein, when Cronjé was expecting further attacks. The standing Boers were protected – both in the open type and in the covered 'shelter trench' pictured above, which gave added protection from shells (Photograph, Dennis Edwards; drawings, *With the Flag*)

Top left General Lord Kitchener, hero of the Sudan, was created a peer after the battle of Omdurman. He accompanied Roberts to South Africa as his Chief of Staff. Cartoon by 'Spy' (*Vanity Fair*)

Top right General Sir Redvers Buller was severely criticised for the British defeat at Colenso. The pomposity of his bearing may explain the dislike of the higher command, but ample proof exists that Buller was well loved by his own men (*British Commanders of the Transvaal*)

Above The Royal Engineers were skilled at constructing emergency pontoon bridges, even under heavy Boer fire (Postcard, Greenwall collection)

Opposite The South African veld had many surprises in store for the British, not least veld fires begun by the Boers. Watercolour by St Leger (Greenwall collection)

prise. His faith in the defensibility of his positions had blinded him to the possibility of Roberts leaving the railway line in his advance. The British were now between Cronjé and the republics; to avoid being cut off, Cronjé was forced to move eastwards as fast as possible.

Cronjé's refusal to rid himself of his cumbersome wagon train made it easy for the British to overtake him. On 18 February Kitchener attacked Cronjé at Paardeberg on the north bank of the Modder River, advancing on three fronts and under cover of heavy artillery fire. Cronjé repulsed Kitchener with minimal losses, while the British lost 1 270 men in what was to be one of the largest casualty totals for a single day during the entire war. Cronjé, however, had suffered a serious setback: so many of his horses and draught animals had been killed in the battle that the wagon laager

could not be moved to safer terrain. He had no alternative but to hold fast to his defensible position and hope for reinforcements to arrive.

In the meantime Roberts and some 40 000 men completely encircled the Boer laager, keeping up a continuous bombardment with his 100 guns. So many men and animals were killed that hygiene and food supplies were seriously affected in the Boer laager. In the appalling conditions that ensued, more than 4 000 burghers and some 60 women and children accompanying them were overcome with despair.

Christiaan de Wet, who was now entering the limelight with lightning attacks on Roberts' convoys, next attempted to relieve Cronjé. De Wet's strategy aimed at Cronjé and his force crossing to the south bank of the Modder River, whereupon he and Cronjé together would break through

Stratford E. Sherman

Highlanders in South Africa adopted khaki aprons to camouflage bright kilts and sporrans (Denis Godfrey collection)

Right The military balloon was widely used by the British in the early stages of the war for reconnaissance. Here the advance on Potgieter's Drift is stage-managed from an advantageous height (*With the Flag*)

the British lines in the southeast, with de Wet covering Cronjé's withdrawal.

With immense daring the Boer scout Danie Theron stole through the British lines to bring this message to Cronjé. But Cronjé's battle-weary officers were not prepared to attempt a crossing of the flooded river. Overruled by his council of war, Cronjé had no alternative but to surrender to Roberts on 27 February 1900 with 4 000 men.

If de Wet had assessed the situation correctly and forced a gap through the enemy lines on the north bank of the river, Cronjé could probably have been relieved without needing to cross the flooded river at all. His surrender was a heavy blow to the republican forces; many of the burghers fled in terror. On 7 March de Wet tried in vain to block the advance of Roberts' overwhelmingly superior force at Poplar Grove. Three days later the burghers under de la Rey offered courageous resistance at Abrahamskraal, but in the end were forced to retreat before the British could succeed in their attempts to encircle them. On 13 March 1900 Roberts entered Bloemfontein without meeting resistance. The Free State Govern-

ment had meanwhile moved its seat to Kroonstad.

On the Cape front, with the support of numerous sympathetic Cape Afrikaners, the Boer force might have been able to prevent Roberts' invasion of the Free State. But instead of launching powerful attacks on Roberts' lines of communication, the Boers tried to halt his overwhelming force with frontal attacks. Eventually they had to fall back through the eastern Free State in scattered commandos.

In the meantime White was tenaciously holding out at Ladysmith on the Natal front. Since early November the Boers, under hesitant officers such as Joubert, Marthinus Prinsloo and Daniel Erasmus, had made only a single and unsuccessful attempt to take Ladysmith. However, relief for the besieged British was on the way.

After his defeat at Vaalkrans, Buller had at last realised that the key to success at Ladysmith lay in taking Hlangwane Hill and the surrounding kopjes, a chain of hills south of the Tugela River and northeast of Colenso, where the vulnerable left flank of Botha's force lay. Buller's capture of these hills between 17 and 19 February signalled the effectual collapse of Boer resistance in Natal. Many burghers left the front, although those who stayed offered valiant resistance to Buller's onslaught. Spurred on by the news of Cronjé's surrender on 27 February 1900, the British on that day

eventually succeeded in breaking through at Pietershoogte. The Boer forces around Ladysmith fell back to the Biggarsberg and the Drakenberg, and on 28 February 1900 the town was at last relieved.

The second British offensive had succeeded on all fronts, and Roberts and Buller allowed their men a well-earned rest. The Boer leaders took the opportunity to re-organise their scattered commandos.

From Bloemfontein to Pretoria

The catastrophe that had befallen Cronjé and his cumbersome wagon laager had taught the Boer leaders a valuable lesson. At a joint council of war of the two republics at Kroonstad on 17 March 1900, a decision was taken to abolish wagon laagers and employ mounted commandos in future. Though the question of wagon laagers was never completely resolved, the decision heralded a new method of warfare which gave the Boers increased mobility. The transitionary phase lasted until the end of August 1900, when the last fixed battles were fought and guerrilla warfare came into its own.

Even before the death of General Piet Joubert on 27 March 1900, dynamic Boer leaders had emerged in the persons of Christiaan de Wet, Louis Botha and Koos de la Rey. As acting Commandant-General, Botha succeeded Joubert as chief of the ZAR forces.

De Wet, now Chief Commandant in the Free State, became the most important exponent of the new style of mobile warfare. For the rest of the war he was to harass the British by attacking from the rear. His favoured targets were the isolated British columns Roberts had spread throughout the south and southeast Free State in order to bring the area under his control.

After de Wet had granted the Free State burghers brief leave of absence, they regrouped in large numbers at the Sand River on 25 March 1900, inspired with new courage.

With his attack on the Bloemfontein waterworks at Sannaspos, 28 km east of the Free State capital, de Wet achieved one of his most brilliant victories. On the morning of 31 March his brother General Piet de Wet opened fire on the British camp at Sannaspos from the east. The British, withdrawing hastily in the direction of Bloemfontein, ran into the ambush prepared for them by Christiaan de Wet, lying in wait with 350 men at Koringspruitdrift. In the ensuing battle the British force under Brigadier-General R. G. Broadwood suffered 159 casualties, while 373 were taken prisoner. De Wet had lost 13 men but had captured a convoy of 116 wagons and a large quantity of ammunition.

The Boers occupied the waterworks at Sannaspos for a considerable time. The water shortage in Bloemfontein contributed to the outbreak of typhus amongst the British soldiers in the town. This definitely contributed to delaying Roberts' advance to Pretoria. After the reverses of the preceding weeks, the victory at Sannaspos raised the moral of the Boer forces, and many burghers who had gone home after the fall of Bloemfontein now took up arms again.

On 4 April de Wet continued his counter-offensive. In a sharp clash at Mostertshoek near Reddersburg, he took 459 British soldiers as prisoners of war. With the exception of the town of Wepener, the entire southern Free State between the railway line and the border of Basutoland was now cleared of British troops. But at this point, instead of concentrating on cutting off Roberts' lines of communi-cation with the Cape Colony, de Wet decided to lay siege to the strategically unimportant Wepener. After an unsuccessful siege of 16 days, the Boers were forced to retire on the arrival of reinforcements for the British troops on 25 April.

April and May 1900 were confusing months for the Boer forces on all fronts. Although many burghers lost courage and returned home to lay down arms, others rejoined the commandos, encouraged by the successes of de Wet in particular. Lack of discipline among the Boer forces was most noticeable at this time.

In these circumstances Roberts again took the initiative. With Pretoria as his ultimate objective, he left Bloemfontein on 3 May with a force of more than 100 000 troops, advancing northwards on both sides of the railway line. His columns were strung out from Kimberley in the west, under Methuen and Hunter, to Buller's forces at Ladysmith in the east.

With barely 8 000 men Botha, who had come over from the Natal front, attempted with de Wet to halt Roberts at the Sand River. Unacquainted with Roberts' tactics of encirclement, Botha on 10 May found French slipping round to the west of his right flank. The Boer force was obliged to fall back to avoid being attacked from the rear. Two days later Roberts entered Kroonstad.

The Free State government moved its seat consecutively to Heilbron, Frankfort and then Bethlehem. The Boer leaders agreed that Botha was to return to the ZAR with the Transvaal commandos, while the Free Staters were to move off to the east — which would afford the republicans the opportunity of attacking the enemy from the front as well as from the rear.

Roberts continued his advance without encountering significant resistance. By occupying the most strategic points along the railway line between Bloemfontein and Pretoria, he considered himself in a position to annex the Free State as the Orange River Colony on 24 May 1900 — Queen Victoria's birthday.

Three days later Roberts invaded the ZAR. Though Lieutenant-General Ian Hamilton suffered heavy losses on 29 May when he clashed with de la Rey at Doornkop, the Boers were un-

Christiaan de Wet, the Boer general who was to become a legend during the guerrilla stages of the war for his ability to elude his more numerous pursuers. At 45 de Wet was short, stocky and grey-bearded, with keen eyes and a markedly silent manner (*L'Illustration*, 1900)

25

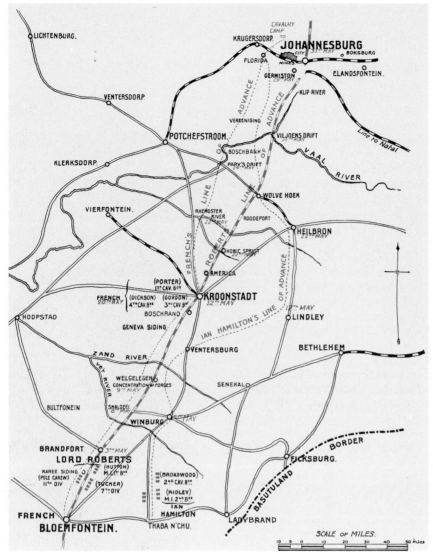

Top left Roberts' advance on Pretoria, shown in a contemporary map. Pretoria was taken unopposed on 5 June 1900 (*Transvaal War*)

Top right The seven month siege of Mafeking was relieved by Colonel Plumer in May 1900, and the name of Colonel Robert Baden-Powell became a byword for British pluck and resourcefulness. Souvenier newspaper celebrating the Relief (Greenwall collection)

Opposite, top 'Charge of the Devons' at Platrand, near Ladysmith on 6 January 1900. The British repulsed an attack by the Boers, who are shown retreating to regroup lower down the slope. The difference between British 'over the top' tactics and the movements of smaller parties of Boers at first gave rise to the notion that the Boers were running away. But in due course the British were obliged to reassess their military methods. Watercolour by W. T. Maud (Greenwall collection)

Chocolate and tobacco for Tommy in the field. Queen Victoria sent her well known tin at Christmas, while the tobacco for Scottish soldiers celebrated Hogmanay. In these splendid examples of memorabilia, the contents of both tins remain well preserved (Greenwall collection)

able to prevent Johannesburg and the Witwatersrand goldmines from falling into British hands two days later. The Transvaal leaders had decided that they would not defend Pretoria, and Roberts entered the capital unopposed on 5 June. Kruger and the government had departed a week earlier, travelling eastwards along the Delagoa Bay railway line to Machadodorp.

Some contemporary observers felt that it was Roberts' long periods of preparation before his advances from Bloemfontein and Kroonstad that had opened the way for the guerrilla phase of the war. But in the light of modern experience of guerrilla warfare, it is now more readily accepted that nothing Roberts could have done could have prevented the transition from conventional methods of warfare to guerrilla tactics.

The success of Roberts' advance once more gave rise to irresolution among the government, officers and burghers of the Transvaal. In an exchange of telegrams on 31 May and 1 June, Kruger and Botha informed their Free State counterparts that the Transvaal officers regarded the continuation of the war as pointless. Steyn and de Wet, however, stood firm and insisted on continuing the struggle.

The guerrilla war is launched

Roberts, who had thought the war over with the occupation of Pretoria, soon realised that the Boers intended to continue their resistance. There were too many areas still not under British control, and the line of communication through the Free State was poorly guarded and vulnerable. Events in the eastern Free State proved the point. On 29 May General A. J. de Villiers dealt General Sir Leslie Rundle a serious blow at Biddulphsberg near Senekal and General Piet de Wet followed up the success two days later against the Imperial Yeomanry at Lindley. It was more than clear that the Free Staters were not prepared to give up the struggle.

The vulnerability of Roberts' line of communication is perhaps best illustrated by Christiaan de Wet's raid on Roodewal Station to the north of Kroonstad. Due to the destruction of bridges by the Boers, large stocks of British supplies and ammunition were accumulated at Roodewal. On the way to Roodewal, de Wet captured a supplies convoy destined for Heilbron on 4 June. Three days later he struck at three places along the railway line, including Roodewal station. The attacks were a complete surprise for the British detachments. Besides losing large quantities of cloth-

Johannesburg was occupied by Roberts in May 1900, ensuring British control of the coveted Witwatersrand goldmines. A military officer photographed the British troops riding into the town (*Khaki in South Africa*)

ing and ammunition worth £100 000 destined for the front, Roberts found himself in telegraphic isolation in recently occupied Pretoria. Within nine days the Free Staters had taken some 1 300 British prisoners of war.

It was clear to Roberts that he had to counter de Wet's operations. He followed up his proclamations of 31 May and 1 June 1900, issued to discourage the burghers and force them to surrender, with another 'paper bomb' on 16 June: if the Boers destroyed rail and telegraph connections, homesteads in the vicinity of such strikes would be burned down. That very morning de Wet's homestead near Roodewal was razed by fire. Roberts was in fact legalising by proclamation a punitive measure that had been applied sporadically since January 1900. Thus the 'scorched earth' policy was not, as is often thought, launched by Kitchener in 1901.

Roberts now made a determined attempt to drive de Wet and the Free State Boers eastwards, hoping to crush them in a pincers-style movement. Bethlehem fell on 7 July after an engagement lasting two days. The Free State government and commandos were forced to fall back behind the Witteberg Range in the Brandwater basin on the border of Basutoland. Here Fouriesburg was to be the last seat of the government before it functioned 'in the field'.

Before Lieutenant-General Sir Archibald Hunter could close off the cordon around the Free State forces, de Wet and President Steyn slipped past Hunter and escaped from the Brandwater area on 15 July 1900, taking with them the Free State government and 2 000 men. The rest of the Free State commandos were to leave the mountains in three groups, each taking a different direction. While dissension over leadership broke out among the Boers, Hunter occupied the exit passes and by the time Marthinus Prinsloo had gained the upper hand, the British were already upon

them. On 30 July Prinsloo surrendered with some 4 400 burghers – half the Free Staters in the field. A further 1 500 men under Chief Commandant Piet Fourie eluded the net at the last moment.

For the time being Fourie was unable to join de Wet. Roberts concluded that he might be able to end the war if he succeeded in capturing de Wet, and initiated the large-scale chase since known as the 'first de Wet hunt'. British columns from all quarters joined in the hunt until there were more than 50 000 men mustered against the elusive Boer general.

With the British in hot pursuit, de Wet raced across the Free State with the aim of continually disrupting Roberts' lines of communication. In this effort Commandant Danie Theron and his corps of Boer scouts, the TVK (Theron se Verkenningskorps), were extremely successful while de Wet was laagered near Vredefort on the Vaal. Across the river General Piet Liebenberg with a Transvaal commando was equally successful on the Potchefstroom-Krugersdorp railway line.

Just in time de Wet succeeded in evading the cordon Kitchener was throwing around him at the Vaal. He and his men were forced into the ZAR and only succeeded in eluding the British on 14 August by crossing the Magaliesberg at Olifantsnek near Rustenburg.

Excellent strategy, combined with mobility, strict discipline and the efficiency of the scouts led by Danie Theron and Captain Gideon Scheepers, were largely responsible for de Wet's success. The weakness of the British communications and intelligence systems, as well as their disrupted supplies, were also to de Wet's advantage.

North of the Magaliesberg, President Steyn and the Free State government left de Wet in order to pay a long overdue visit to President Kruger in the eastern Transvaal. At Waterval Onder the executive councils of the two republics decided in a joint session on 28 August to send the ageing President Kruger via Delagoa Bay to Europe, where he was to seek the intervention of European governments to secure peace with the preservation of independence for the republics.

Schalk Burger was appointed Acting President of the ZAR.

Meanwhile de Wet had left his main force resting and had personally set out for the Free State with 246 burghers. At the Magaliesberg British columns caught him in a semi-circle from which he could only escape across the mountains, in what proved to be one of his most famous escapes.

An important result of the first de Wet hunt was to delay Roberts' advance from Pretoria along the Delagoa Bay railway line: for a whole month he was forced to concentrate on attempting to capture the Boer general. The hunt was also a watershed in the war. At the urging of their leaders, the burghers to a great extent rid themselves of their cumbersome wagon trains, and conventional trench warfare was exchanged for the mobility of guerrilla warfare. (The Spanish word guerrilla literally means 'small war'.)

Roberts had occupied Pretoria for a week when, on 11 June, he launched an attack on General Botha's 40 km-long line of defence 30 km east of the capital. On the afternoon of 12 June, Lieutenant-General Ian Hamilton broke through the Boer lines on the southern flank at Diamond Hill near Donkerhoek. Under cover of darkness Botha and his force slipped away, leaving Roberts in control of the terrain. Botha and the Transvaal forces fell back eastwards along the railway line to protect their rear against Buller's advance from Natal, thus enabling French to occupy Middelburg on 27 July.

Only when the first de Wet hunt had ended in failure was Roberts able to return his attention to his eastward advance. On 15 August his Middel-burg forces met up with Buller's from Ermelo; the British force now numbered over 20 000. With a mere 5 000 burghers to defend his line, Botha prepared for what was to be the last conventional battle of the war, at Bergendal (Dalmanutha). Here, between 21 and 27 August, the Boers put up a courageous fight with a handful of ZARPS – policemen of the ZAR – bearing the brunt of the attack under heavy bombardment on 27 August. But Roberts' superior artillery finally won the day and Botha was forced to retreat in the direction of Lydenburg.

Convinced that he had crushed the Boers, Roberts annexed the Transvaal to Her Majesty's dominions on 1 September 1900. Three weeks later his columns reached Komatipoort, on the border of Portuguese East Africa. The entire Transvaal south of the Delagoa Bay railway line was now in British hands – or so it appeared. In fact, although Roberts controlled most of the towns and had numerous divisions in the field, his authority reached no farther than the range of his artillery, or the spot where his columns stood at any given moment. As soon as a British column moved off, a commando would return and reinstate Boer authority. The war was far from over.

The guerrilla war entered a new phase when de Wet and Botha began sending the commandos back to their respective home districts, with orders to engage the British whenever the opportunity arose. If the British force were too powerful, the commando was simply to move aside and let it through. Commandos were split into small groups that were easier to conceal; when an isolated British division was sighted, the commando could be re-assembled at lightning speed to mount a surprise attack. Mobility was the key to Boer strategy, with the mounted commandos in a position to be far more active than the laagers of burghers who possessed no horses.

A thorough reorganisation of the Boer forces took place. Capable leaders were appointed, in place of being elected, to replace those who had proved inefficient. Under the new arrangements, burghers who had taken the oath of neutrality and returned to their farms were called up again. The most active organisers were de la Rey in the western Transvaal and de Wet in the Free State, and their efforts and encouragement caused many burghers to rejoin the commandos, to a certain extent compensating for the surrender of Prinsloo in the Free State and the reverses the Transvalers had suffered since the surrender of Cronjé. By September 1900 the war had taken on a character entirely different from that of the preceding year.

For de Wet the adoption of guerrilla tactics heralded a period of reverses.

'British patrol in sight'. Angus McNeill's sketch depicts a Boer fleeing his Cape farm at the approach of a British patrol. The rebel colonist had joined the commandos, returning to his farm when the coast was clear. In the later stages of the war, captured rebels were charged with high treason; 33 were executed (Greenwall collection)

At the battle of Nooitgedacht in the Magaliesberg, December 1900, Boer forces overwhelmed the Northumberlands at the edge of a precipice. The heliograph operator signalled defeat before falling to his death. Wash drawing by F. Waugh (Greenwall collection)

Between 20 and 25 October he and Liebenberg besieged Major-General G. Barton at Frederikstad Station in the western Transvaal, but co-operation among the Boer officers was poor and when Barton's reinforcements arrived the Boers were obliged to beat a retreat, leaving at least 26 of their number dead.

On 1 November President Steyn and the OFS government rejoined de Wet. Five days later the Boer laager was surprised near Bothaville by Lieutenant-Colonel P. le Gallais, who found the Boer sentries fast asleep. Le Gallais died of his wounds that evening, but 114 Boers were taken prisoner. De Wet and Steyn escaped with the rest of the burghers to continue

Boer resistance. Steyn's leadership was a true inspiration to all: he firmly believed that the republican ideal would triumph. He was indeed the soul of the Boers' struggle for freedom.

Attention could at last be given to de Wet's long-cherished ideal of invading the Cape Colony. When the republican forces had been withdrawn from the southern and western fronts in March 1900, the Cape rebels had been left in the lurch. Hope rose that a new invasion would once more encourage Cape Afrikaners to join the Boer forces. In addition, the extension of the theatre of war to the Cape Colony would considerably complicate the task of the British, who would have to withdraw troops from the Free State and Transvaal to ward off the new Boer offensive.

On their way south de Wet and his

1 500 mounted burghers forced the British garrison at Dewetsdorp to surrender on 23 November, and 408 British were taken prisoner. The delay however enabled the British to formulate plans for pursuing the Boers. Three flying columns under General C.E. Knox sped off on the second de Wet hunt, while thousands of troops were despatched by rail from the Transvaal.

Little came of de Wet's plans to invade the Cape Colony in December 1900 with three sections at Hopetown, Colesberg and Aliwal-North, but General J. B. M. Hertzog succeeded in shaking off his pursuers and penetrating to Lamberts Bay on the Atlantic coast. By the end of February 1901 he was back in the Free State.

Heavy rains impeded de Wet and contributed to the failure of his campaign. The Orange River was flooded and across the river British columns stood in wait, while Knox was threatening him from the rear. Privation took a heavy toll of de Wet's men and animals. But his mobility enabled him to escape from the triangle formed by the Basotholand border and the confluence of the Orange and Caledon Rivers. On 14 December 1900 he made his famous breakthrough at Sprinkaansnek near Thaba Nchu, when his burghers dashed through a rain of bullets between two British forts. Commandant P. H. Kritzinger and Gideon Scheepers secretly held back at the Orange River and later operated in the Cape Colony.

De Wet rejected Botha's proposal for a jointly planned strategy of invasion. At the end of January 1901 he made a second attempt to invade the Cape. From all over Kitchener rushed in troops by rail and launched the third de Wet hunt: some 14 000 British troops in 17 flying columns descended upon the Boer force of 3 000 men. De Wet's well-tried ruse of constant feints kept his pursuers confused about his direction of travel, and he crossed the Orange to the west of Philippolis on 10 February 1901. However, lack of grazing for the horses hampered de Wet's mobility. Many burghers had to walk 18 hours a day, carrying their rifles, saddles and blankets. Once again the rains frustrated their plans: de Wet was held back by the flooded Brak River, until on 28 February he was finally able to find a way back into the Free State through the Orange River.

De Wet's second invasion of the Cape Colony was a complete failure. He had failed to rally the Cape Afrikaners to his cause in an operation that had proved his most difficult to date, involving exceptional demands and privations. He had finally lost the strategic initiative, and from this point on would be largely committed to defensive guerrilla warfare.

In the eastern Transvaal a period of comparative calm followed the Battle of Bergendal, since the Boer commandos in general avoided engagement with the numerically superior British force. However, in a nocturnal attack on 28-29 December 1900, General Ben Viljoen overwhelmed an isolated British garrison at Helvetia, near Machadodorp.

In July 1900 de la Rey was delegated to regaining the western Transvaal from the British, and his exceptional ability as administrator and as a general in guerrilla warfare soon became evident. On 11 July he gained a brilliant victory at Silkaatsnek, scarcely 30 km west of Pretoria. This success, heralding the reactivation of Boer resistance in the western Transvaal, attracted large numbers of burghers who had laid down arms back to the commandos.

De la Rey's half-hearted siege between 4 and 16 August of the British camp on the Elands River (where Zwartruggens is today) was a failure. Accompanied by the ZAR State Attorney, J. C. Smuts, de la Rey himself left the siege and proceeded to Zeerust and Lichtenburg. Here he made important civilian arrangements, including appointing magistrates for the area.

In the final months of 1900 de la Rey and the combat-generals under his command constantly harassed the British. On 3 December, to the north of the Magaliesberg, he captured a convoy of 126 wagons bound for Rustenburg with Christmas supplies for the British troops. Ten days later de la Rey and General C. F. Beyers, with 2 500 burghers in all, followed this up with a victory over General R. A. P. Clements at Nooitgedacht.

Clements' camp, comprising 1 500 men, lay in a kloof at Nooitgedacht, at the foot of the southern slopes of the Magaliesberg. On the peak above, some 300 British troops manned a signalling station. Early on the morning of 13 December the Boers attacked from the west – Beyers on the crest of the mountain, and de la Rey and Smuts (recently appointed combat-general) south of the mountain. Beyers' occupation of the peak, which enabled his burghers to fire on the camp in the kloof below, decided the battle. But because Smuts failed to block Clements' line of retreat and de la Rey's men began plundering the British camp, Clements succeeded in escaping with nearly two-thirds of his force. Boer casualties numbered 78, while 332 of the British had been killed or wounded and 306 taken prisoner. The Boers had acquired as booty a large quantity of provisions, draught animals, rifles and ammunition, in a victory that raised the morale of the Transvalers, particularly those in the western districts.

Nooitgedacht was not one of de la Rey's best victories. His attack had not been efficiently co-ordinated with Beyers, and his burghers were still to learn the discipline he was to force upon them in the later stages. Still, de la Rey's planning had been outstanding, his information had been accurate and he knew the terrain. He had also employed two vital principles of warfare: speed and surprise. This paved the way for his success.

Everywhere the guerrilla war was taking root. Boer optimism was mounting, and when Kitchener assumed command from Roberts on 29 November 1900, the war was still far from over.

The final phase

With 210 000 troops at his disposal, Kitchener made every effort to alter an unfavourable military situation. But close on 100 000 of his men were spread out with passive duties along the railway lines or as isolated garrisons. For the guerrilla warfare, the cavalry and mounted infantry were undoubtedly his most important troops. He therefore immediately called for further mounted reinforcements.

Kitchener employed a threefold

Top British-made handkerchief complete with an Anglo-Boer War alphabet (Greenwall collection)

'Colonial Scout', painted by W. S. Cumming. In his slouch hat the colonial soldier looked at home on the veld (Greenwall collection)

strategy to end the war. Firstly, he continued Roberts' scorched earth policy. The republics were subjected to a systematic devastation. Whole towns, as well as thousands of farmhouses, were burned down or extensively damaged. This onslaught on the Boers' means of survival was intensified by the destruction of all food supplies: livestock was killed in enormous numbers, and fields of grain and maize were burned.

As a second strategy, the concentration camp system was extended as more civilians, chiefly women and children, were interned. Thirdly, Kitchener began his 'drives' – a method to drive the commandos out in front of him and trap them against

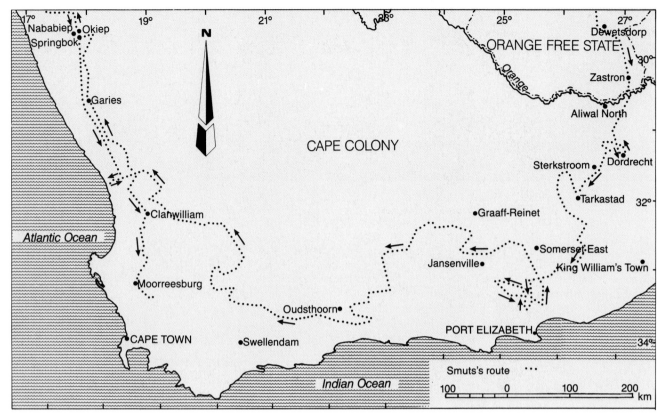

Smuts's daring invasion of the Cape Colony, September 1901 to May 1902, caused widespread alarm in the Cape

lines of blockhouses and barbed wire erected for this purpose in a network spanning the entire theatre of the war.

On 28 January 1901 Kitchener launched the first great drive with seven columns of 14 000 troops and 58 guns. His target was the Transvaal Highveld, between the Delagoa Bay and Natal railway lines. Most of the commandos offered no resistance, since they knew that they were hopelessly outnumbered, but they did succeed in breaking through the British lines in smaller numbers. Behind the lines they were safe for the time being, though the destruction sown by the advancing British brought great shortages of food. Amongst those who broke through the lines was General Louis Botha, who attacked Major-General H. L. Smith-Dorrien at Chrissiesmeer on 6 February. Eventually the British columns had advanced through the districts of Ermelo, Piet Retief, Vryheid and Utrecht until, by the middle of April 1901, they had reached the Natal border.

With winter at hand, a part of the Transvaal that had been prosperous before the war lay devastated. Homesteads had been burned down, farm stock slaughtered or carried off, and most of the civilians sent to concentration camps. Yet the number of burghers eliminated from the battlefield by Kitchener's drives, chiefly through their own voluntary surrender, was insignificant. Out of a total of 132, most were either old or very young – or they were the fainthearted, who were of little use to the Boer cause.

Meanwhile, Kitchener and Botha had met at Middelburg on 28 February 1901 for peace talks, at Kitchener's suggestion. He was fairly lenient in his peace proposals, but his most important demand – that the republics should surrender their independence and become British colonies – was unacceptable to Botha. This ensured the continuation of the war.

Kitchener began extending the application of his scorched earth policy systematically. The Free State and Transvaal were ravaged, so that the winter of 1901 brought the utmost privation to the burghers and their families. The commandos grew less active and avoided any encounter with the

British. Boer women fled into the veld in small groups to avoid being sent to the concentration camps. The commandos, cut off from their sources, supplemented their supplies of food, clothing, rifles and ammunition by attacks on isolated British detachments. The Boers were no longer able to keep prisoners of war, and released them immediately after capture.

In these circumstances despair overtook the Boer leaders, including Acting President Burger. The Free State leaders and others were aggrieved at this loss of courage and on 20 June 1901 President Steyn and Generals de Wet and de la Rey were among those who tried to rally the faint-hearted at Waterval in the Standerton district, calling upon them to continue the struggle to the bitter end. It was also decided that Smuts would lead a new invasion of the Cape Colony to relieve the pressure on the two republics.

Shortly afterwards, in Reitz on 11 July, President Steyn narrowly escaped being captured for a second time. From the documents that fell in British hands, Kitchener learned of the irresolution of the Transvaal government – to him proof that his

Jan Christiaan Smuts, the young and brilliant State Attorney of the Transvaal, proved a bold guerrilla leader (*Onze Krijgsofficieren*)

Left Commandant Gideon Scheepers, drawn from a photo after his capture by the British in the Cape Colony. He was executed, but his grave has never been found (*Heroes*)

scorched earth policy was bearing fruit. But his proclamation of 7 August 1901, stating that officers who refused to lay down their arms before 15 September would be banished from South Africa and their possessions confiscated, failed however to achieve the desired effect.

In the meantime the resistance of Kritzinger and Scheepers in the Cape Colony was stimulated by the arrival of small commandos under Fouché, Lategan, Wynand Malan, Jan Theron and Manie Maritz. In May 1901 Kitchener sent French to the Cape Colony. With Middelburg as his headquarters, French was to use his 50 000 troops to eliminate the roughly 3 000 burghers, who were dispersed over a wide and difficult terrain, and were active from Aliwal North in the east to Port Nolloth in the west, and from Philipstown in the north to very near Cape Town in the south.

French's task became even more difficult when in September 1901 Smuts crossed the Orange River near Aliwal North with 250 men, taking the struggle in the Cape into a new phase. The Colony was to be part of the theatre of war to the end.

Smuts was harassed continuously on his journey, which took him first towards the Eastern Province, then the southwestern districts and eventually to the northwestern districts of the Cape. Early in January 1902 he met up with Manie Maritz in the northwest Cape. With General J. van Deventer, they took the offensive in the vicinity of Okiep, occupying Springbok and Concordia in April 1902.

The British authorities declared martial law in the Cape Colony, removing draught animals from the farms and punishing rebels severely. But this did not deter Cape Afrikaners from offering the invading commandos their hospitality and assisting them in their difficult mission. The war had placed the Cape Afrikaners in a serious dilemma. Though most of them did not hesitate to affirm their loyalty to the Crown publicly, and to make it clear to the invading republican forces that their presence was embarrassing, Cape Afrikaners were often bound to the republicans by blood and cultural ties. The war was therefore for them a great source of affliction.

Though the majority of Cape Afrikaners chose the path of loyal resistance in the Boer struggle for independence, there were several thousand who joined the invading commandos as rebels. They were swayed not only by sympathy with the Boer cause but by false claims by the commandos, and even by force. The poor administration of martial law in some districts was a further factor. A total of 12 828 Cape Afrikaners were ultimately brought to court on charges of high treason, of whom 9 747 were found guilty. This represented about 10 per cent of the whites in the Cape. On the other hand, more than 12 000 Cape colonists had joined the Cape police and the volunteers' corps, on the British side, by December 1900.

In the Free State the guerrilla war was still characterised by Boer attacks on isolated British detachments, patrols and convoys. But the British were now also deploying cavalry and 'bagging' smaller commandos in nocturnal attacks. Before dawn on 25 December 1901 de Wet launched a highly successful attack on the British column on the crest of Groenkop, between Bethlehem and Harrismith. Some 500 burghers swarmed up the steep and poorly guarded western slope of the hill and overwhelmed the 470 British soldiers in their sleep.

De Wet continued to evade capture, despite the resources massed against him. Here, as he attempts to cross the railway line, he meets fierce fire from blockhouse and armoured train alike (*Transvaal War*)

Among the 58 British who were killed was the commander, Major F. Williams. The Boers found the food and ammunition taken as booty a welcome Christmas gift.

It was at this stage that Kitchener introduced his 'new model drives'. More blockhouses had been erected and he was now in a position to co-ordinate his drives more efficiently. These in fact became great sweeps during which his columns, stretched out in lines easily 80 km long, ousted the Boers from the theatre of the war.

During February and March 1902, Kitchener deployed as many as 30 000 troops and several armoured trains in three attempts to trap de Wet against the railway line in the northeastern Free State. Though Kitchener did not succeed in catching as many Boers as he had hoped, the new model drives were a success. The constant pursuit had an adverse effect on Boer morale, and the British destroyed food sup-

plies as they swept across the land. With the winter of 1902 approaching, this became a serious factor in the duration of the struggle.

After the meeting held at Waterval on 20 June 1901, Louis Botha organised an invasion of Natal in September, in order to divert some of the British columns from the Transvaal. But with the Buffalo River in spate, and the British deploying troops, for Botha to invade Natal with 2 000 burghers became an impossibility. He did, however, successfully put the Boers' new 'stormjaag' tactics (mounted attacks) into operation against a British column at Blood River Poort on 17 September. Despite his attacks on the British posts at Itala and Fort Prospect nine days later, Botha was still unable to break through to his targets in Natal. By early October 1901 he and his commandos were back on the Transvaal Highveld. Though his attempted raid on Natal had failed, Botha had shown that the Eastern Transvalers were still an active force in the field.

On 30 October 1901 Botha compensated for his reverse in Natal when he once again mustered his commandos with impressive speed and won a 'stormjaag' victory at Bakenlaagte over the capable Lieutenant-Colonel G. E. Benson's isolated column. Benson, who had been harassing the commandos in the eastern Transvaal by their own methods, was fatally wounded in this attack. Though there were still to be many more skirmishes in the eastern Transvaal, they had little effect on the outcome of the war.

In the western Transvaal the approach of the spring of 1901 heralded a busy time for both sides. One after the other, British commanders were sent out to capture de la Rey. All of them – Methuen, Babington, Dixon, Cunningham, Clements and Kekewich included – had to sound the retreat with some losses. At the start of 1902 Methuen was still hunting de la Rey, whose mobility had been severely limited by Kitchener's blockhouse lines. The British, assisted everywhere by 'joiners' (Boers who had crossed to the British side), were now also setting out on great nocturnal drives to round up the Boers. However, de la Rey successfully employed the 'stormjaag' technique on the British when they were on the move, as shown at Yzerspruit on 25 February 1902. Colonel Anderson lost 183 men, killed or wounded; the 500 taken prisoner by de la Rey were released the next day.

The Battle of Tweebosch on the Little Harts River on 7 March 1902 once more proved de la Rey's aptitude as a cavalry commander. His veterans stormed the rearguard of Methuen's convoy in mounted formation, firing from the saddle with deadly accuracy. It was de la Rey's most brilliant victory.

The Boer losses of 34 were small in comparison with the 189 British soldiers wounded or killed and the 859 taken prisoner. Methuen, wounded in the leg, fell into Boer hands, but with characteristic magnanimity de la Rey released him so that he could obtain better medical attention than the Boers were able to offer.

Victory in the Battle of Roodewal near the Harts River on 11 April 1902 went to the British. With de la Rey engaged in the peace talks, General J. Kemp attempted to storm the combined forces of Colonels Grenfell, Kekewich and Von Donop but was beaten off. Some of the Boers were taken prisoner, 43 died and 120 were wounded. Roodewal was the last important battle of the war.

Peace

Peace came after two years and close on eight months of war. The first move was a missive from the Dutch Prime Minister, Dr Abraham Kuyper, sent to the British government on 25 January 1902 and offering his government's services as mediator for an interchange of thoughts on peace between Britain and the two republics. Kitchener sent copies of his correspondence on the subject to the Transvaal government, though not to the Free State government. The outcome was that the two Boer governments met at Klerksdorp on 9 April and with Kitchener in Pretoria three days later. It was decided that the burghers still in the field should elect a number of delegates to meet at Vereeniging on 15 May and decide whether to enter into peace negotiations with the British, with or without recognition of the independence of the republics.

Between 15 and 17 May 60 delegates from the Transvaal and Free State commandos held talks under the chairmanship of General Beyers at Vereeniging. President Steyn, who had contracted a muscular paralysis, attended only one or two of the meetings. Some of the delegates were in favour of surrender, while others insisted on continuing the struggle. The plight of the women and children in the concentration camps; the increasing threat posed by armed blacks to both the burghers on commando and to Boer families roaming the veld; the devastation of the land in the two republics and the resultant shortage of food – all these were powerful arguments for ending the war.

Representatives of the two republican governments submitted the delegates' proposals to Kitchener and Milner in Pretoria on 19 May. The most important was the republics' readiness to sever their foreign ties and accept a British protectorate. Kitchener and Milner firmly refused to conduct negotiations on any basis but the complete surrender of their independence by both republics.

Smuts and Hertzog proceeded to work out terms of peace with Milner. On 21 May their proposals were sent to Britain for government approval. These provided for the burghers on commando to lay down their arms and acknowledge Edward VII as their sovereign. Prisoners of war would be repatriated to the Transvaal and the Orange River Colony, provided they took the oath of allegiance to the Crown, in which case they would be allowed to retain their personal possessions and their freedom. The Dutch language would be taught at school and permitted in the courts. As soon as circumstances allowed, self-government would be granted to the Transvaal and the Orange River Colony, and the issue of black enfranchisement would not be decided before the former republics attained self-government. Britain would make a sum of £3 million available for the reconstruction of the two devastated regions.

Between 29 and 31 May the Boer delegates met again at Vereeniging. At length with heavy hearts they voted 54 for, and 6 against, the peace terms formulated in Pretoria.

The members of the two Boer governments thereupon travelled to Pretoria, where at about 11 o'clock on the evening of 31 May 1902, the Peace Treaty of Vereeniging was signed in Melrose House. 'We are good friends now,' said Kitchener, extending his hand to the Boer delegates. Friends, perhaps – but for the Boers it was a peace without freedom.

'Peace – with Honour'. The British postcard features Chamberlain's portrait and a cameo of the soldier's homecoming (Greenwall collection)

Bottom By the end of the war, Queen Victoria had been succeeded by her son Edward, seen here as Colonel of the 10th Hussars. He refused to be crowned until peace was signed (*Transvaal War*)

CHAPTER 3

The Tommy in South Africa

They called him 'Tommy Atkins' – the typical British private, who was of necessity drawn from the British working class. Rudyard Kipling's ballads had created a popular image of a hardened though sometimes sentimental man, a loyal fighter who lacked education and polish but was, in the end, endearingly human.

Over the centuries the British army had been built up into a formidable fighting machine consisting of a Regular Army as well as volunteers and militia recruited specifically for the war effort. A strong surge of British imperialism, or rather of aggressive nationalism, had brought the Unionist (Conservative) party into power in Great Britain in 1895. Added to the widespread belief that the British were the best people in the world, patriotism inevitably played a rôle in the brisk enlistment of troops for South Africa. Among the working class, however, it was a less powerful motivation, even though most of the recruits to the Regular Army were manual labourers. In 1898 only 7,3 per cent of recruits were from the lower middle class (shop assistants and clerks), while a mere 1,1 per cent were professional people of the middle class.

Many recruits enlisted in the Regular Army to counter unemployment. Privates were paid five shillings a day, Sundays included, which offered security and a steady income – a motivation emphasised by the fact that enlistment in the Regular Army tended to be seasonal. In summer, when employment was more plentiful and it was not too cold to sleep in the open, enlistment was negligible; those who did enlist in summer were in many cases unable to find other work, or were simply work-shy. But joining the army was not always a last resort. Many enlisted because they liked soldiering and adventure and wanted to see new parts of the world.

Like the Boers, the Tommies arrived at the South African front not really knowing what to expect. They sailed from British ports amid scenes of great enthusiasm and a good deal of merriment. 'We are off to have a shot at old Kruger,' were the parting words of many a recruit. The voyage itself was an ordeal. 'A ship is a prison with a chance of being drowned,' someone remarked. Inadequate ventilation on the steamships and poor food gave rise to many diseases and even deaths at sea. Lectures were held throughout the voyage to prepare the Tommies for their struggle with 'the Boer'.

Each soldier was issued with a khaki uniform. The word khaki is derived from the Hindustani word meaning 'dust' or 'dusty'. The Tommy's uniform consisted of a jacket, trousers gathered below the knee, khaki leggings and brown boots, a khaki helmet and other headgear, and a khaki overcoat. He was issued with a rifle and bayonet, a bandolier, rucksack and water bottle, and a canvas kitbag for his personal possessions: a blanket, warm shirts, socks and underwear, brushes, shaving kit, a pocket knife and the sewing kit popularly known as a 'housewife'.

There were clear class distinctions in the army. Traditionally the professional officers came from the upper class, as their titles frequently testify. In a world already tending towards egalitarianism, most officers insisted on the proper maintenance of class differentiation. The middle class in the main provided volunteer contingents such as the City Imperial Volunteers and the Imperial Yeomanry; it was this social group that tended to believe in everyone being treated alike and suffering the same privations – a view not shared by the ordinary Tommy, who came from the lowest class of all.

The relationship between aristocratic officers and the working class Tommy did however move towards greater equality as the war progressed. In the first phase of conventional warfare, the officers were both physically and socially removed from the troops. In their quarters they mixed only with their social peers, and it was only during military action that they had any real contact with their troops. But as the war entered its guerrilla phase in 1900, and smaller, more mobile patrols became common, officers and men drew closer to one another and social differences were blurred.

Everyone slept on the hard ground and endured the same blazing heat or bitter cold in their pursuit of the mobile enemy. Leadership now rested less on the officer's rank than on his personal qualities. Officers who were strict but just, and who showed concern for the needs of their troops, were immensely popular.

Psychologically speaking, the British Tommy was sober about the events of the war, and sometimes even somewhat bitter and cynical. Generally he endured with stoicism the privations of war far from home in a foreign country, with its extremes of temperature. There were exceptions, of course, such as the private who lost his mind and roamed the veld southeast of Pretoria stark naked during May 1902. Boers who went in search of the man found him suffering from extreme exposure. Though they gave him a blanket and food, all the demented man could say was 'Where are they?' Peace came shortly afterwards, and what happened to the man is only conjecture.

Several religious denominations were represented in the Regular Army: 68,6 per cent of the men were Anglicans, 17,6 per cent Roman Catholic, 7,5 per cent Presbyterian, 5,3 per cent Wesleyan and 0,7 per cent from other denominations. Though the average Tommy had great respect for the chaplains and particularly for those who shared his hardships in the field, he made no great display of religion. A war artist with the British forces noted that he had never heard a Tommy singing a hymn, whether alone or in company, nor did he ever hear any reference to religion in the conversations of officers or men. In defence, a chaplain deplored the narrow interpretation of the word 'religion' and insisted that, though the number of religious men among the Tommies might be small, it compared fairly well with the number among civilians of the same class. Soldiers, he said, might appear to be uninterested in religion when they were not on active service, but in times of war their thoughts turned instinctively to God.

Soldiers who made a display of their religious convictions were often mocked, but a man who had proved himself the equal of his comrades in

war was usually left in peace. The Tommy's religion was not without its humour: a regiment that had marched 160 km greeted the chaplain's announcement of the Sunday hymn, 'Art thou weary?' with a half-suppressed chorus of 'Yes!'

Christmas brought the British troops gifts from Home: the traditional Christmas pudding and, as in 1899, tins of chocolate 'with the compliments of Queen Victoria'. While the Boers emphasised the religious character of the day, Christmas in the British camps appears to have been a more light-hearted, festive occasion. In 1899 the Boers fired two dud shells engraved with 'The compliments of the season' into Ladysmith – one, humorously, contained a piece of Christmas pudding.

Schooled as they were in British 'race patriotism', the Tommies were not surprisingly openly hostile towards the Boers. The author Bill Nasson has claimed that many of the troops shot at the Boers with undisguised enthusiasm, and quotes a

soldier who wrote: 'The boys were all high spirited, telling one another how they bayonetted and shot the Boers.' Vastly outnumbered, the Boers were forced to fight a retreating war, often giving way before impossible odds in order to live to fight another day. The Tommies, not understanding this, branded the Boers as cowards – an underestimation Tommy would often have cause to regret.

Tales of both kind and cruel treatment of Boer wounded and prisoners of war have been recorded. Generally, the British treated such Boers well, an experience also shared by most Boer women. In the few instances of rape or assault of Boer women by British soldiers, the culprits were severely punished. The burning of home-

Inset, above Tommies on guard in the streets of Johannesburg take a resourceful break for luncheon (Cape Archives)

Below A sergeant recruits for the British army in London's Trafalgar Square (*L'Illustration*, January 1900)

Above Tommy's Christmas under Southern African stars, vividly captured in this watercolour by H. Collison Morley (Greenwall collection)

Below 'Pipers of the 2nd Black Watch in South African kit' (postcard, Greenwall collection), and 'Colour-Sergeant and Private in Khaki, Gloucester Regiment' (*Transvaal War*)

Opposite Postcards alternately glorifying or poking fun at Tommy Atkins in South Africa; the tiny soldier's bible designed to fit in the tunic pocket; a unique hand-painted envelope celebrating 'the Gentleman in Khaki ordered south'; and a silk song-sheet of the words that inspired it (Kipling gave his royalties from *The Absent-minded Beggar* to the Daily Mail Fund for reservists' wives and children). Above the song-sheet is the flattish oval tin each Tommy carried as his emergency ration. It contained 4 oz concentrated beef and 4 oz cocoa paste, calculated 'to maintain strength for 36 hours if eaten in small quantities' (Greenwall collection)

steads was official British policy, but the execution of such orders, whether with aggression or with reluctance, varied from one patrol to the next. Many Tommies regarded Boer women with some physical distaste – a reaction mainly to the 'bywoner' or backward type.

British military methods during the conventional phase of the war showed scant regard for the need for shelter. British columns were therefore often surprised by a Boer attack while they were still in closed formation, as at Magersfontein. The Tommies found the South African veld a strange terrain, where taking aim was a particular problem, but with time their expertise in the veld increased. In the guerrilla phase of the war the long marches, often by night, were extremely exhausting for the Tommies. During drives on Boer commandos British enthusiasm generally ran high, but reverses and persistent failure, as experienced against de Wet and de la Rey, caused immense frustration. Patriotic pride in the superior British army was not always enough to sustain the Tommy; like the Boer, he frequently put self-preservation first. When the Boers opened lethal fire on a regiment, as at Magersfontein and Colenso, many a Tommy ran away, or refused to charge the Boer positions.

Letters to relatives at home, however, reveal that the British soldier often fought with great spirit. A Welshman wrote to his parents: 'You can't believe how happy I was fighting against the Boers. I felt as if I were in a football match.' A Scot from the Gordon Highlanders wrote home: 'We charged three times with the bayonet, and my gun was covered with blood, although I don't remember striking anybody; but I was nearly mad with excitement – shells bursting, and bullets whizzing round like hail. ' It was not unusual to hear Tommies, who bitterly recalled the British

God Bless you Tommy Atkins, here's your country's love to you.

TOM.B.

ACTIVE SERVICE.

At Duty's Call

GRUSS VOM KRIEGSSCHAUPLATZ

Der englische Zinnsoldat
unter der Sonne Afrikas.
„Wenn Menschen aus-

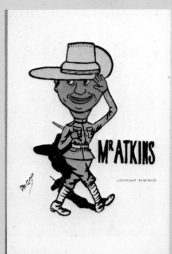

Mr ATKINS

COPYRIGHT RESERVED

SOLDIER'S NEW TESTAMENT

SOUTH AFRICA 1900

Welcome to the brave Commander
of that band of Heroes
The Natal Field Force.

ONE SHILLING 1901

"For the Gentleman in khaki ordered South."

"He's left a lot of little things behind him."

"There are girls he walked with casual,"

"Doing his country's work."

Mr A Clark, 25 Seaford Road, South Tottenham, London

£185

THE ABSENT-MINDED BEGGAR

BY

RUDYARD KIPLING.

defeat of 1881, storming the hills with vengeful yells of 'Majuba!'

The British army imposed a firm discipline on its troops. In contrast with the Boer system, this left the individual British soldier little scope for initiative. When an officer commanding an operation was put out of action, the troops were in many instances thrown into confusion and were even afraid of giving the command to alter rifle-range. Though the Tommy grumbled at unpopular commands, he generally accepted them philosophically enough. 'It's all in the seven,' he would say, referring to his seven year service in the Regular Army.

British soldiers had come from a land of gentle greens, and South Africa with its extremes of temperatures and seasons held little charm for them. The dry, dusty veld made them long for home and many diary entries complain of the bitter cold, particularly during Highveld winters. 'The

cold at nights is so bitter and searching that we can hardly sleep, lying in the open as we do, and one does not get warmed through again by the sun until 10 or 11 in the morning,' one Tommy wrote. The British army was poorly equipped: the thin canvas tents, when they were available, gave little shelter, while a single blanket, often shared by two men, provided barely any warmth during cold Highveld nights. The heat of the northwest Cape and Free State was another field hazard for the British, whose skins were unaccustomed to the blazing sun. Kilted Highlanders pinned down by Boer fire at Magersfontein were badly sunburned on the bend of their knees.

Inadequate food supplies were a source of constant grumbling. Meals were announced by a bugle call, but the daily menu consisted of little more than tinned bully beef or oily ham, a smoked herring spread, four

rock-hard biscuits, and occasionally a little jam. In the guerrilla phase of the war even this frugal meal was not always available. On tough expeditions half-rations sapped the strength of the troops. Few British columns learned to live off the veld, as the Boers did. Orchards offered welcome relief, but many a Tommy learned the painful way that it was unwise to stuff his shirt front with prickly pears!

A Tommy wrote home: 'Please lay in a huge supply of food before I come, or I know I shall eat the house out, especially porridge.' He went on to describe how he and his mate would torment each other on the march with huge imaginary feasts. 'Roast beef and potatoes!' his mate would say, and he would chime in with 'Peas and Yorkshire pudding!'

The scarcity of food encouraged looting, as did the long periods of comparative idleness, the soldiers' freedom of movement in small patrols, and the application of the official scorched earth policy. Looting by individual soldiers, for instance on the battlefield, was uncommon. But joint looting of Boer and black property by British patrols occurred on a large scale; poultry, dairy products, and cattle and sheep were particularly likely to be taken.

Action against drunkenness and disorderly behaviour increased as the war dragged on, and the army authorities became reluctant to hand out the official tot of rum to stir the fighting spirit of the troops. The problem was

aggravated when the Tommies found ways of obtaining locally brewed alcohol. Drinking undermined not only discipline but the Tommy's fighting spirit and his fitness, and those found guilty of excess were severely punished – two privates were for instance sentenced to 112 days of hard labour. According to a chaplain, 22 per cent of the Regular Army were teetotallers.

Relaxation in the field was an important facet of British army life. The men often played cards and a game called Check was particularly popular, played with buttons on small cloth squares of different colours. Organised and spontaneous sports were important pastimes: cricket, rugby and soccer promoted team spirit, while games played on horseback were also highly popular – after one battle the British troops held races with horses taken from the Boers. Scorpion racing and betting were other favourites, as well as tug-of-war and various exuberant races: obstacle, three-legged, wheelbarrow & even egg-and-spoon. At night an easy camaraderie reigned around the camp fires.

The Tommies' sense of humour was irrepressible even in the most difficult of circumstances. A group was once boiling water for tea when a Boer fusillade sent them rushing for shelter. When the water boiled, one of the Tommies leaped out and risked his life to fetch the kettle, before calmly proceeding to

make the tea. Tommy humour was quick, with a ready answer for everything.

Sentry duty around the camp was often extremely boring, particularly at night when the dark hours dragged by painfully slowly. Every half-hour the silence was broken with cries of 'Number!' and 'All's well!' Sometimes the British were caught off-guard, especially by nocturnal Boer attacks.

Despite reasonably adequate medical facilities, enteric fever and associated diseases took a high toll of British soldiers, generally as a result of poor hygiene and food. It is striking that several Boer diaries mention the fact that the Tommies had lice; Boer commandos also refused to spend a night on an old British camp site for fear of both infestation and infection. Enteric fever and dysentery cost many lives, particularly in besieged towns such as Ladysmith, where 393 of the troops died from them. Bloemfontein soon overtook Ladysmith's tally of 10 mortalities a day, with the Raadsaal serving as hospital. Disease had first gained its hold when soldiers drank polluted water from the Modder River at Paardeberg. Neglect of sanitary precautions in the British camps promoted the spread of enteric fever, which also took its toll in poorly managed field hospitals such as the one at Kroonstad.

Not all British regiments stayed in South Africa for the entire duration of the war; those that returned to Britain

were replaced by fresh regiments. In general, going home was a source of great jubilation to the Tommy. Some chose to remain behind and seek their fortunes in South Africa, but most could barely wait to return to their families and the green fields of home. On the South African veld, 22 000 British graves testified to the horror of war.

The photographs and paintings were legion that recorded the British experience in South Africa

Opposite Tommies take their morning wash in the Orange River (Dennis Edwards), and on their off day play a game of cards (*War Pictures*)

Above Shooting partridges from an armoured train provides one of war's lighter moments, while the elegance of his picnic distinguishes General Bruce Hamilton's luncheon at Spitzkop, Natal (Greenwall collection; *After Pretoria*)

Below The unwanted distinction of being 'third man' guarding horses during action – and thus a conspicuous target. By I. Sheldon-Williams (Greenwall collection)

On commando

CHAPTER 4

Le Petit Journal

SUPPLÉMENT ILLUSTRÉ

Le Petit Journal

Le Supplément illustré

Huit pages : CINQ centimes

ABONNEMENTS

Onzième année   DIMANCHE 14 JANVIER 1900   Numéro 478

LA GUERRE AU TRANSVAAL
Le général Joubert haranguant les Boers

When by late September 1899 it had become clear that war was inevitable, the Boer leaders called up 56 to 65 per cent of their burghers between the ages of 16 and 60 for military duty. Preparations for the war had begun much earlier. Every burgher kept his rifle carefully oiled, his bandolier filled and his horse stabled. Commando law laid down that each burgher had to keep in constant readiness a horse, his saddle and bridle, a rifle and 30 bullets and enough food for eight days; thereafter the state would provide for him, though indigent burghers received state help from the outset.

The Boers wore no uniforms and set out on commando in their workaday clothes: corduroy trousers, shirt and jacket, broad-brimmed hat and home-made veldskoens. Generals, commandants and field-cornets also wore civilian dress and as a result could not be distinguished by their clothes. A Boer setting out on commando carried everything he would need in his saddle-bags or tied in bundles to the saddle. Generally his equipment included a blanket, a sheet of canvas to provide shelter, a three-legged cooking pot, a kettle and bags of flour, salt, biltong and rusks.

The Boers were ready to leave im-

In this French portrayal of General Joubert addressing his men, the magnificence of his uniform is a colourful but inaccurate touch (*Le Petit Journal*, 1900)

Close combat was not the Boers' favourite form of fighting; they had a justifiably morbid fear of British bayonets. Fred Waugh's dramatic 'Defence of a trench' (Greenwall collection)

mediately the call-up came – some riding off with anxiety, others to rash boasts of 'chasing the English into the sea'. In many cases three generations of a family set out together: father, son and grandfather. Despite the age limit, it was not uncommon to see boys of 12, 13 and even younger, as well as greybeards of between 70 and 80 on commando.

When individual burghers had formed their commando at a pre-arranged spot, the mounted company were ready to move off to the front. Commando members who lived far from the front, for example in Pretoria and Johannesburg, merely caught a train at the nearest station. Who were these burghers, and what was their outlook on life as they rode off to battle, with their rifles over their shoulders? Generally, they were men sustained by the deep conviction that they were setting out to fight for God, their country and their freedom. They were devout Calvinists who believed in the justness of their cause,

as reflected in manifestos published by the governments of both republics at the outbreak of war. Steyn concluded his manifesto with the words: 'To the God of our fathers we humbly commend the justice of our cause. May He protect what is right: May He bless our weapons; under His banner we march into battle for freedom and fatherland!'

The Boers did not separate politics from religion, and it was not uncommon for them to sing their national anthems or other patriotic songs at religious services in the field. They believed with simple faith in the will of God, as Boer diaries kept on commando testify. They identified themselves as a nation with the Israelites, the chosen people of the Old Testament. In a sermon in the field on Sunday, 15 July 1900, the Reverend Paul Roux took his text from Isaiah 66:8: 'Shall a land be born in one day? Shall a nation be brought forth in one moment?'

Military success or failure, or the

successful conclusion of a difficult river crossing, was frequently followed by a prayer or a hymn. Thanksgiving services and prayer meetings were regularly held in the laagers and were continued during the guerrilla phase when the Boers perforce had to operate in smaller groups. For most of the burghers the Bible was a source of inspiration and they read it constantly, referring in their diaries to Bible texts drawn particularly from the Old Testament. Biblical references also occur in official Boer telegrams, and Boer victories were attributed to the presence of 'the God of our fathers'.

Boers on commando received regular visits from the ministers of the three Dutch churches, the best known of these spiritual leaders being the Reverend J.D. Kestell of Harrismith, who spent much time in the laager with de Wet and Steyn. The

Burghers at prayer, with the umbrellas so many Boers carried with them on commando for convenient shade (Cape Archives)

sabbath was observed by the Boers as the traditional day of rest and in the early days of the war no preparations for battle were made on this day, though circumstances forced the Boers to relax this custom during the guerrilla phase.

Visitors to Boer laagers were struck by the spiritual conviction of the Boers, and noticed in particular the evening prayers held by small groups of the burghers. However, they had faint praise for the Boers' ability to sing, a German volunteer remarking that it would be torture for any music lover to listen to them, while a Russian ambulance sister serving on the Boer side declared: 'The sound was unharmonious, but they sang with great inspiration and the effect at night and in such circumstances was a powerful one.'[5]

The Boers drew great strength from their faith, which formed the cornerstone of their national spirit. Yet there were some who drifted away from their religious ideals. Towards the end of the war the Reverend J.P. Liebenberg noted in his diary: 'And if the dear Lord should not sorrow over us! With all our anxiety and affliction there is still so much sin: disobedience and lack of faith, vanity and apostasy.' The Reverend A.P. Burger regarded the lapsed believers as a minority group who 'merely formed the plasterwork of the solid building of the Afrikaner people'.[6]

Though private property was generally respected by the Boers, burghers occasionally looted shops and houses belonging to people who did not support the Boer cause. Drunkenness also occurred, though the Boers were generally moderate drinkers who regarded the occasional bottle of brandy or whisky coming their way as a welcome bonus. De Wet claimed that the Boers were no drunkards and added: 'On the contrary, when compared with other nations, they are remarkable for their sobriety, and it is considered by them a disgrace for a man to be drunk.'[7]

Discipline among the Boers was more of a problem. Of all the Boer generals de Wet was best known for the discipline he enforced, though even he stated that true discipline was non-existent among the Boers. He once remarked, somewhat cautiously, 'I do not intend to imply that the burghers were unwilling or unruly, it was only that they were quite unaccustomed to being under orders.'[8] One of the reasons for the lack of discipline was that the Boers, with their pioneering background, were individualists accustomed to solving their own problems. They had always acted on their own initiative, particularly in difficult circumstances, and were not used to receiving orders from somebody else. On their farms, each man had been master, and in a way each Boer saw himself as a general. He knew the veld, and he had developed the knack of coping for himself in all circumstances.

At the beginning of the war this stubbornness occasionally delayed battles while groups of Boers argued the date of attack. But as the war progressed, discipline improved. The 'bittereinders' (bitter enders) were deeply committed to the war, and the Boer force was therefore gradually purified of its unwilling burghers, who had either surrendered or had joined the British army.

Leave, and absence without leave, were two phenomena the Boer leaders found vexing. On many occasions burghers grew tired of life in the laagers and departed with or without permission to visit their homes, only to turn up again a few days later on commando. Boer leaders spoke of the 'leave pest' but it should be borne in mind that the burghers were nothing else but farmers, husbands and fathers, serving in a people's army. Whenever the Boer forces fared poorly on the battlefield, the 'leave pest' struck harder.

One of the clearest results of the lack of Boer discipline was the hindrance caused by cumbersome wagon laagers, a problem experienced by all the Boer generals. At the beginning of the war many burghers took all kinds of luxuries on commando, including iron bedsteads, mattresses and stoves, which were piled onto the wagons and transported from site to site. Loading and unloading, the constant inspanning and outspanning, all delayed the Boers' movements. The encumbrance of a large wagon laager was one of the reasons for the surrender of Cronjé and his 4 000 men on 27 February 1900 at Paardeberg. Soon after, the Boer officers decided to send most of the wagons back to the farms, and by September 1900 most of the wagon laagers had been broken up and the luxuries dispersed. Wagons were used well into the guerrilla phase, however, and even at the end of the war were still hampering mobility. One of the reasons for the Boers' attachment to their wagons was the feeling that they were all they had left once the British began burning their homes and removing their wives and children to the concentration camps.

Breaches of discipline did not entirely go unpunished by the Boers. Burghers disobeying orders and for instance shooting buck in the veld were severely punished. One form of punishment was 'paksaal', which meant the offender had to walk around the laager for hours with his saddle, rifle, bandolier and bridle on his head, suffering the derision of his fellows. Another punishment was 'beesvel ry' (literally, riding oxhide). The offender was roughly helped onto the bloody hide of a freshly slaughtered ox. Holes cut along the edges of the hide provided firm handholds for a number of men who shot the offender up into the air, amid loud merriment. As soon as the culprit touched down, he was thrown up again until he was judged to have suffered enough and the cheering onlookers were satisfied.

Though the burghers tended to cherish too great a sense of individual independence and lacked strict discipline, they were to a great extent dependent on certain leaders who had won their confidence – particularly men of the calibre of de Wet, Botha and de la Rey. The Boers felt free to discuss everything under the sun with their commanders, and a foreign commentator was once an astonished witness to a burgher approaching Commandant-General Piet Joubert, head of the Boer forces, to ask for shoe-laces. Boer leaders frequently gave rousing speeches, urging the burghers on to great determination.

On commando there were always necessary tasks to be performed, including sentry duty or 'brandwag staan', with a group of 30 burghers positioned about half an hour's walk from the laager behind breastworks of rock, corrugated iron and sandbags. There they would wait for the night, wrapped in blankets and with their rifles at the ready. After prayers and psalms the burghers took turns to stand guard through the night, as a Boer recorded: 'At night we stand guard in pairs, while the others sleep next to the horses at the foot of the ridge. We are not allowed to stand upright, but crouch at the tip of the ridge so that we have a good view of anything approaching without being seen ourselves.'

Another task was reconnoitring, which was adventurous but dangerous work. Their life in the veld had made some Boers superior scouts, accounting for much of the success on the Boer side. By night or day, they were skilled at gathering valuable information about the movements of the British while remaining undetected. Although ordinary burghers also acted as scouts, the specialised scouting corps won particular renown, especially Commandant Danie Theron's corps, known as the TVK (Theron se Verkenningskorps). Theron himself won fame for his heroism crawling to and fro through the British lines in order to take a message from de Wet to the beleaguered Cronje.

Despatch riding or 'rapport ry' was also dangerous and highly responsible work. Confidential messages and communications between officers were delivered by experienced riders who knew the South African veld so well that they were able to slip through British lines unseen.

The Boers were naturally completely dependent on their horses, and took great care of them though at times they rode them hard. The Boer horse was a tougher animal and better acclimatised than the horses brought by the British from Britain, Australia and the Argentine. At night the Boers kept their horses close to their sides in readiness for a quick getaway. If there was not enough fodder, the horses were usually knee-haltered (hobbled) in an enclosure to allow them to graze without wandering too far.

For the Boers, a normal day outside times of combat saw some burghers returning from sentry duty soon after sunrise for their first cup of coffee with rusks. As the war progressed and the Portuguese closed Delagoa Bay to imports, coffee became a rare luxury and supplies were supplemented by the roasted roots of a species of wild fig tree, or by 'coffee' ground from wheat, mealies or sweet potatoes. Water was plentiful, particularly in the rainy season, though the burghers in the northwestern Cape experienced severe shortages in this arid region. Sugar had been a scarcity from the first few months of the war.

After coffee, one burgher would be appointed as cook for the day for each group of five or six men. The staple food was mealie porridge, bread and meat, which was roasted, boiled or dried as biltong. The vetkoek, doughy griddle cakes made from flour, were humorously dubbed 'stormjaers' or 'maagbomme' (stomach bombs). When an ox was slaughtered, a 'meat corporal' would divide up the meat by standing with his back to the burghers and handing out the meat without looking at the men. Complaints were strictly forbidden.

This Boer bandolier (*left*) forms a complete waistcoat, ornamented with the numbers and badges of various British regiments – presumably as trophies (*Heroes*)

Below Boers drying biltong in camp – a habit of great interest to foreign observers (*L'Illustration*)

Ingenious substitutes were invented for imported articles. 'Everything was scarce, but nothing was completely lacking,' the Boers later claimed. Soap was made from the ash of mealie stalks. Salt, always a very scarce item, was scraped from dry salt-pans. Mills to grind wheat were transported on the wagons, and mealies or wheat were secretly planted in patches in the mountains; these harvests were hidden for later use.

As the years went on, clothing became a severe problem that was only partly alleviated by trousers, jackets and shoes manufactured from the hides and skins of slaughtered oxen and sheep. By the winter of 1901 the process of 'uitskud' (literally, shaking out) had become expedient: captured British soldiers were only released when the Boers had 'shaken' them out of their clothes. Many burghers ended the war dressed in an assortment of British military wear. British supply convoys provided further largesse in the form of loot. 'As long as there are British soldiers in South Africa, the Boers will have enough supplies,' is how a volunteer with the Boers summed up the situation.[9] In the final phases of the war many burghers were shooting with Lee-Metfords taken from the British.

On non-combat days spent quietly in the laagers, the Boers did their various chores but also found time for traditional games such as tug-of-war, quoits, rugby, athletics, cricket and boxing – the latter either bare-fisted sparring or a matter of knocking the hat from your opponent's head. On New Year's Day and other special occasions they held Boer sports, putting up valuable prizes: on New Year's Day, 1902, at a sports meeting near Heidelberg in the eastern Transvaal, the prize in the three-legged race was a pipeful of tobacco for winners, while the victor in the long-jump event was rewarded with enough mealie coffee for a cup or two. Each member of the winning tug-of-war team received a pinch of snuff. Shortly before the end of the war the Boers planned a rugby match against the British. Manie Maritz's commando near Okiep was all set to play Colonel Sheldon's men, until a senior British officer called off the match. Peace was concluded barely a month later.

The Boers' supper was eaten round the camp fire. Afterwards, someone would produce a guitar or a violin and the rest of the evening would be spent singing religious or popular songs. At length each man would wrap himself up, fully dressed, in a blanket or an overcoat and lie down on his bed of grass, with his head on his saddle and his rifle ready at his side.

An examination of the social distinctions in force among the Boers on commando reveals the paradox of fiercely independent burghers who yet relied with the greatest trust on a powerful military leader. Equality was a feature of Boer social life, and those social differences that did exist were seldom strictly applied. Yet there was clearly a Boer aristocracy, and a certain measure of privilege. General Ben Viljoen made a significant comment when he said of two burghers: 'They belonged to the Boer aristocracy, members of honourable families whose high birth and qualities had secured for them preference over thousands of other men and the unlimited confidence of the Head of State.'[10] While the Boer aristocrat, the ordinary burgher and the humble by-woner were all exposed to the same hardship, the more affluent burghers were decidedly better off. When Ver Loren van Themaat, an upper-middle-class volunteer, lost his horse, he remarked: 'As an infantryman you cannot achieve anything; you do not belong in the Boer forces and you are always in the company of Afrikaners of a lesser quality'[11] – by which he meant the poorer Afrikaners.

The state of sanitation in the Boer laagers provoked a fair amount of contemporary comment. A. G. Hales, the *Daily News* correspondent, stated that the Boers were careless and ignorant of even the basic principles of the laws of sanitation. 'I did not see a single latrine in any of their laagers,' he wrote, 'nor do I think they are in the habit of making them, and to this cause and to no other I attribute the large amount of fever in their ranks.' A German volunteer on the Boer side

explained that the Boers simply left the laager and walked until out of sight, to avoid being seen. H. R. Davis, a British war correspondent, described the Boers as 'foul and unkempt', but also recorded burghers bathing in a river. Hales probably offered a fair comment: 'It is true that in their laagers one does not see much soap and water used as in our camps, but this is possibly due to want of opportunity as much as to want of inclination.'[12]

Jan Celliers, the well-known Afrikaans poet, was an articulate witness to the Boer's spiritual experience in the war. After only a few days on commando, he wrote: 'Our entire lifestyle has been changed and much is lacking. Yet I and many others feel that we may not complain.' He went on to describe how dirty and dusty everything was, and portrayed the rough society of his bearded, unkempt fellow burghers who had been re-leased from the restraining influence of their womenfolk. A year later, in October 1900, Celliers pointed out that commando life had stripped the burghers of 'everything that was part of their humanity', until only the core remained. Now, he felt, they would know themselves and their fellow-men better.[13]

Life on commando was a training ground in human relationships. For two and a half years men who had been accustomed to being masters on their own farms were thrown roughly together. The war obliged them to co-operate with each other and resign themselves to accepting orders. As the struggle proceeded, many of the burghers attained greater calm and resignation; others became indifferent, particularly in the face of repeated setbacks. Ver Loren van Themaat remarked: 'One no longer asks what the future will bring. In due course we shall find out.'

Initially any Boer camp in the field was a fairly substantial laager consisting of ox wagons and mule-drawn carts, as shown in F. Waugh's wash drawing above. Intended for reproduction in Britain, the picture is entitled 'A Hurried Inspan' and shows a laager moving on under threat of attack. Boer mobility was severely hampered by the necessity of loading and inspanning such wagons and carts. Cronjé's surrender at Paardeberg in February 1900 was partly due to the large wagon laager under his command. From then on, wagons were increasingly frowned upon on commando, though some Boers persisted in using them (Greenwall collection)

Opposite page, left In this German postcard of Boers firing on the British, though the fighting style is faithfully depicted, liberties have been taken with the burghers' clothing. The Boers tended to wear subdued colours, and it was only the men of the Staats Artillerie, in the early stages of the war, who wore a formal uniform (Greenwall collection)

Opposite, right By the end of the war, the Boers had developed effective cavalry charges, especially under de la Rey, as for example at the battle of Tweebosch in the Western Transvaal (*Die Buren*)

How did the Boers react to battle? A member of the Pretoria commando, awaiting a British attack towards the end of 1899, noted in his diary how calm his fellow Boers were, even though they knew full well that they were being threatened by a force far superior in numbers. A year later, when his commando was preparing for the battle at Nooitgedacht after months of idleness, he himself experienced a 'sort of raging, excited courage to take on anything'.[14]

It was the battles on the Tugela front, where the Boers had a clear view of the enemy marching upon them, that left the deepest impression. In hand-to-hand combat, as at Spionkop and Nooitgedacht, there was little time to think about the battle. Conventional set-piece engagements gave the burghers the opportunity to inquire after each other's welfare and to comment on the course of the battle. Most Boers had a horror of the lances of the British

cavalryman, probably due to gruesome tales of the cavalry action at Elandslaagte. But the initial fear of bombardment soon gave way to indifference. When the Boers realised, for instance, that the lyddite shells used by the British were not particularly dangerous, they began joking during bombardments and refusing to take shelter. But 'bombs are still bombs', a rather more cautious Boer reminded his comrades, whose levity no doubt concealed the same fear.

The experience of death, whether of comrades or of British soldiers, initially shocked many Boers. But in time even a man as sensitive as Jan Celliers came to remark that the grim sight of the fallen dead had begun to seem commonplace – though he hated this acquired callousness.

Like the Tommies, the burghers endured a constant struggle with the elements. Biting cold, torrential rain and hail, scorching heat and troublesome winds took their toll on the patriotism of the burghers. Proof that they grew accustomed to it all, however, comes from an entry in the diary of a burgher six weeks before peace was concluded: 'But all these vicissitudes of nature do not intimidate us any longer.'[15]

When peace came, it was a saddening experience for those Boers still in the field. They found it hard to believe that they were now British subjects. Some of them wept openly, others exclaimed that they had lost their faith in God; most however retained that faith – their loss of freedom was His will and He would ensure that justice would prevail. At last it was time to go home. But the Boers found their farms virtually razed to the ground, and they faced the daunting task of beginning all over again. Only when all the men had returned from commando or had been repatriated from prisoner of war camps overseas, and when the women and children had come back from the concentration camps, were the families finally reunited. At the family tables, empty chairs bore silent testimony to the dead.

War transformed farmers' sons into sombre fighting men (Dennis Godfrey collection)

CHAPTER 5

Boer prisoners of war

From early on in the war, the British had to make provision for the accommodation of Boer prisoners of war. Eventually as many as 20 000 Boer prisoners were held in the various camps, which should not be confused with the so-called concentration camps intended chiefly for the Boer women and children, but to which blacks were also sent.

Transportation and the supply of food for Boer prisoners were perennial problems. The journey to the nearest suitable railway station had to be undertaken on foot, a great hardship for old men and young boys, before the prisoners made their uncomfortable train journey to the camps. They were often treated in a humiliating fashion by their guards on these journeys, and found the mockery of black bystanders along the way hard to bear. Entries in diaries do however mention many instances of courteous and humane treatment of Boer prisoners of war.

The prisoner of war camps in South Africa lay far from the theatre of war, so as to prevent interference by Boer commandos. In Natal there were camps at Umbilo and Tin Town, a transit camp at Ladysmith. In the Cape camps were established at Bellevue in Simonstown and at Green Point in Cape Town, the latter being the largest prisoner of war

Right General Piet Cronjé spent most of the war as prisoner on St Helena (*Heroes*)

Above Boer prisoners on board the *Penelope* at Simonstown (*De Vrijheids-Oorlog*)

camp in South Africa. While Bellevue was being completed, prisoners were kept on cargo vessels in extremely uncomfortable conditions.

Mass surrenders, particularly by Cronjé with some 4 000 burghers and Prinsloo with 4 400, meant that the South African camps were soon flooded. The presence of republican and rebel forces in the Cape Colony increased the vulnerability of the camps, and led the British to consider shipping prisoners to camps in various parts of the Empire. Escapes would be eliminated, and it was hoped that the psychological effect of the removals would contribute to the capitulation of the Boer forces. Camps were consequently constructed on the Bermudas, in India and on the islands of Ceylon (Sri Lanka) and St Helena.

The Bermudas are situated in the Atlantic Ocean some 900 km from the North American mainland, halfway between the West Indies and Canada. Camps were built on eight of these small islands, and here the prisoners were accommodated in tents. The camps were not fenced with barbed wire, as others elsewhere were. More than 4 600 Boers were held prisoner of war on the Bermudas from July 1901 till after the end of the war.

On mountainous St Helena, the is-land to which Napoleon had been banished in 1815, some 5 500 Boer prisoners of war were located in the Deadwood and Broadbottom camps, in tents so crowded that the men soon began building their own huts. A third and smaller camp was built on the island for prisoners of war who had taken the oath of neutrality or allegiance to the British Crown during the war.

Ceylon contributed five camps, the best known being Diyatalawa, approximately 300 km to the east of the capital Colombo and the largest of all the camps on the island: it accommodated some 5 000 Boer prisoners of war. The first group of prisoners arrived at Diyatalawa in August 1900. Ragama was a smaller camp, but so overcrowded that it swiftly became the most hated camp in Ceylon.

In India 17 camps were erected, from the far south up to the foothills of the Himalayas, with Trichnopoly and Shahjahanpur the best known. Conditions in the Indian camps were the most unpleasant the Boer prisoners of war experienced; dry, burning heat and wind exacerbated the discomfort of the men.

The voyage into the unknown was a severe trial for most Boer prisoners. 'Oh, it is a heavy task to leave our beloved country in this manner,' one of them noted. In many cases the prisoners did not even know where they were being sent, which increased their despair. Sometimes the guards taunted the prisoners, jesting that they would never be allowed to return to their homeland. Boer officers were generally well treated, but the burghers, relegated to the stifling holds of the ships, suffered great discomfort. Most of the ships were dirty and infested with vermin, and what food there was was poor, with the result that periodic epidemics broke out. Many deaths consequently occurred at sea. The monotony of the voyage did little to alleviate the prisoners' misery.

Each prisoner of war camp fell under the supervision of a British camp commander, who controlled provisions, discipline, medical services and postal and sanitary arrangements. The British military authorities generally provided inferior and inadequate food, but this was a matter beyond the camp commander's control. Sanitary arrangements on the whole were good, but the organisation of postal services was criticised, particularly the stringent censorship imposed by the British, which caused long delays – a common cause for complaint in a situation where mail day was a major event.

Camp hospitals were often full, and fellow prisoners of war assisted with the nursing of the sick. The prisoners elected their own hut captains, line captains and corporals. Discipline was strictly maintained in all camps, though treatment of the prisoners varied with the nature of those in charge. According to S.P.R. Oosthuizen, the treatment varied from brutal and arrogant to courteous, sympathetic and humane.

Confinement under guard was a

Above Mortimer Menpes, author and artist, described the long dusty lines of Boers taken prisoner at Paardeberg in February 1900 as one of the most moving sights of the war. The surrender of such a large number (4 000 at Paardeberg alone) meant that transit camps in Natal and particularly Cape Town were soon flooded, leading to some of the prisoners being kept on cargo vessels in Simonstown harbour. Original watercolour painted by Menpes for his book *War Impressions* (Greenwall collection)

Opposite page, left The main Cape prisoner of war camp was situated in the sports stadium at Greenpoint. This hand painted postcard provides a simple but effective portrait of the solemn rows of tents (Greenwall collection)

Opposite, right Postcards of St Helena soon included mention of the Boer prisoners of war. Shown on this map are Deadwood Camp, Broadbottom Camp and General Cronjé's residence in exile, Kent House (Greenwall collection)

sore trial for Boers who were used to the wide open spaces of the South African veld. They found it difficult to accept the restriction of movement, the monotonous routine of military discipline, and their enforced idleness. In such a concentration of men there was naturally social friction, while longings for home and family, and the uncertainty of their return, weighed heavily on the men. Camp life, however, demanded that the prisoner of war surrender his individuality to the common good, creating a recognition of group identity that helped him to endure the privations of camp life.

The Boer's innate sense of humour often came to the rescue, relieving tension. Soon the camps took on the appearance of small villages with an organised way of life. From Ceylon an observer wrote: 'This Boer community as I soon discovered, controlled by their own officers, manage every-

thing for themselves, having among them their own tradesmen and artificers of every sort, their shops and their schools and churches, all within the limits of the wire enclosure.'[16]

Most Boer prisoners found that confinement deepened their religious faith, with visible effect on their attitudes and conduct, and helped them to submit to camp discipline. Various religious societies were formed, such as De Christelijke Strevers Vereeniging. Some of their ministers had been taken prisoner on the battlefield and transported with them, but in cases where there were no ministers the prisoners themselves took the initiative. Large catechism classes were held in all the camps – often the only formal schooling the prisoners had ever received.

Many of the Boer prisoners regarded captivity as punishment for their sins, and a certain degree of fanaticism emerged; the Reverend Paul

Boys were frequently among the prisoners taken in the guerrilla stages of the war. These, photographed at Madras in India, had been captured in the eastern Transvaal in December 1901 and January 1902 (*After Pretoria*)

Below right One of the camp newspapers produced at Deadwood, St Helena (Greenwall)

Roux remarked that there was 'possibly too much religion and too little devotion'.[17] Religious principles had their advantages: there were no differences of rank or class amongst the Boer prisoners, and in general they showed little hatred of the enemy who had put them in their situation.

Besides those Boers taken prisoner in battle, some non-combatants or 'huislêers' (literally, house-liers) also found their way to the camps. Young boys, some only eight years old but most of them between 12 and 16, had frequently been taken prisoner either with their fathers or in the veld where they had been herding stock; they were also sent to the camps, along with old men, many of them in poor health.

There were those among the Boers who took the oath of neutrality or the oath of allegiance soon after their capture. Renegades supplied the camp authorities with information on their fellow prisoners' political views and plans for escape. As their numbers increased, these informers aggravated political division in the camps. Burgher peace committees visited the South African camps from time to time and persuaded further prisoners to take the oath of allegiance, while their assistants canvassed the camps abroad. S. P. R. Oosthuizen states that this development 'cast a permanent shadow on the lives of the prisoners of war, since it led to mutual distrust, enmity and division'.[18] In fact, it frequently led to fisticuffs and assault. The 'oorlopers', those who crossed over to the British side, enjoyed the protection of the camp authorities, while the leaders of the uncompromising die-hards were subjected to punitive measures such as solitary confinement, greatly increasing the bitterness among the prisoners of war.

Free time in the camps was used for organised sports such as rugby, cricket, athletics, tennis and boxing, which were enjoyed by participants and spectators alike and proved a sound antidote to boredom and self-pity. Debating societies aired subjects ranging from 'Is the death penalty desirable?' to 'Was the attitude adopted by the Cape Colony in the war just and reasonable?' Music societies and choirs, including the Christy Minstrel Entertainment at Green Point camp, were other lively cultural activities.

Camp newspapers reported news of camp events; a well-known paper was *Kamp Kruimels* (Camp Crumbs), first issued on 20 December 1900 in Deadwood camp, St Helena, and handwritten on wax sheets for duplication. On 8 June 1901 Deadwood produced the first edition of a second newspaper, *De Krijgsgevangene*, while the best known newspaper in Diyatalawa, Ceylon, was called *De Prikkeldraad* (Barbed Wire).

Handcrafts were a popular pastime and prisoners made a large variety of articles from soft slate, wood, bone and sometimes ivory: anything from walking sticks, pen handles and pipes to napkin rings and brooches.

In most camps schools were founded for the younger prisoners, run by ministers and those prisoners who had been teachers in civilian life. Soon older prisoners joined in as well – for many of them this was their first and only opportunity to receive a formal education. Though hampered by the shortage of textbooks and stationery, the schools made a great educational contribution.

Attempted escapes from the camps were naturally common, given the practical bent and initiative of the Boers and the severe frustration of confinement. Besides special excursions, the prisoners were only allowed freedom of movement within

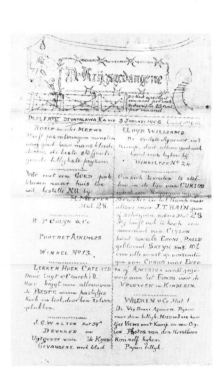

Deadwood Camp, St Helena, had a well
established air by 1901, when this picture was
taken, showing the ingenious homes and shops
manufactured from biscuit tins in Blikjesdorp (Tin
Town). The camp newspaper opposite advertises
various enterprises ranging from printers to tailors
and the cheerful Lekker Hoek Cafe (Greenwall
collection)

the barbed wire fences surrounding
the camps; guards were instructed to
shoot anyone attempting to escape.

Few escape attempts succeeded.
Some Boer prisoners had escaped in
South Africa while travelling by train
to their respective camps: Commandant C. J. Spruyt of Heidelberg, for
example, rejoined his commando after great hardship, only to die on the
battlefield 18 months later. A mere 20
to 30 Boers succeeded in escaping
from camps overseas. They made
their way to friendly countries, but
only a few managed to return to
South Africa and take up arms again.
St Helena, Ceylon and the Bermudas, as islands, offered as little hope
of escape as the camps deep in the interior of India.

Perhaps the most remarkable Boer
escapes were those of J. L. de Villiers
from Trichnopoly in India, and Willie
Steyn with his four companions from
the harbour of Colombo, Ceylon. De
Villiers had noticed that each afternoon an Indian with his cart passed
through the camp gate without attracting attention. Laying his plans
carefully, De Villiers disguised himself as an Indian and walked out of
the gate, past the guards, to catch a
train to the first station in French territory in India. The book he wrote

about his experiences was translated
from the original Dutch into Afrikaans in 1934 and published under
the title *Hoe ek ontsnap het*.

Willie Steyn and his companions
made an even more daring escape.
After several near-successful attempts at escaping from Green Point
camp, they jumped overboard in the
harbour of Colombo. A Russian ship
picked up all five men and took them
through the Black Sea to St Petersburg, where the enthusiastically pro-
Boer Russians fêted the escapees.
From St Petersburg the men travelled
via Berlin to Utrecht in the Netherlands, visiting President Kruger before sailing from Hamburg for German South West Africa. Eventually,
after over a year's absence, all but one
of the party rejoined the Boer commandos east of Calvinia. Tragically
one of the four men, Piet Botha, died
shortly afterwards of wounds received in a skirmish. The story of the
escape was subsequently published
by L. A. Visagie under the title *Terug
na Kommando*.

In the camps the prisoners greeted
the announcement of peace with jubilation. A diarist on Ceylon noted
that his whole camp was in a tumult
of joy, with national anthems ringing
out and thanksgiving services held in
various huts. Even the British guards
expressed their joy by cheering as the
orchestra marched through the
camp. But the first reports had not de-
tailed the conditions of peace. Boer

prisoners generally had believed so
firmly that they would win the war
that they had not dreamed that peace
would rob them of their independence; the reality came as a tremendous shock. Prisoners were obliged
to take the oath of allegiance to the
British Crown before they were allowed to return to South Africa. For
many this meant a serious moral
struggle, so that taking the oath was
an extremely painful experience for
them. Others refused to take the oath
and remained in Bermuda, or settled
in the United States and the Argentine.

As early as July and August 1902,
the first of the transport ships carrying jubilant ex-prisoners back to
South Africa set sail. Other prisoners
were to wait considerably longer to
see the land of their birth again. Jan
Celliers' poem best conveys the experience of homecoming.

> *Gold,*
> *blue:*
> *veld,*
> *sky;*
> *and one bird wheeling lonely, high—*
> *that's all.*
>
> *An exile come back*
> *from over the sea;*
> *a grave in the grass,*
> *a tear breaking free;*
> *that's all.*

(Translated by Guy Butler)

CHAPTER 6

Women and children in the war

At the outbreak of war, most Boer women remained on the farms and tried with their children's help to continue farming. Others, faced with a shortage of food and clothing and fearing attacks by neighbouring black tribes, settled in the towns.

During the period while the British forces were still halted on the borders of the republics, Boer women played an important complementary role to the men on commando, giving them both spiritual and material support. Messages, letters and parcels of food and clothing continually found their way through to the Boers at the front. But with the invasion of the western Free State by Roberts in March 1900, and Buller's invasion of the ZAR from Natal in July 1900, the material aid the women were able to give their men on the front declined sharply. From this point on the measures introduced by Roberts, and by Kitchener after him, determined the fate of the Boer women and children. For most of them the road led to the concentration camps. Other women deliberately avoided the British columns and roamed the veld.

The scorched earth policy

As early as January 1900, before the arrival of Roberts in South Africa, troops under Major-General J. M. Babington burned down farm homesteads in the western Free State. In his proclamation of February 1900 Roberts himself expressed disapproval of the destruction of property and of the molestation of civilians by his forces.

This and his subsequent proclamations were aimed at persuading the burghers to lay down their arms.

During Roberts' invasion of the Free State and his occupation of Bloemfontein in March 1900, on the whole the British columns left the Boer homesteads and the women and children in peace, though they confiscated all available horses and supplies of fodder and maize. Early in May 1900 Roberts continued his northward advance through the Free State. The Transvaal leaders decided to leave the women and children on the farms, as had been done in the Free State, rather than bring them up behind the front lines. Transportation difficulties, and the refusal of the women to leave, would in any case have made evacuation impossible.

Between the occupation of Bloemfontein and the taking of Pretoria, several farm houses were burned and plundered – mainly by the Colonial Division, consisting chiefly of volunteers from the Eastern Cape under the command of Brigadier-General E. Brabant. Though these actions were contrary to his orders, Roberts does not appear to have voiced any particular objections.

The Hague Convention of 1899 determined that the destruction of property was to be limited to what was 'imperatively demanded by the necessities of war'. Roberts was acting within these limits during the period March to June 1900 when he authorised the destruction of all homesteads from which Boer snipers fired on British troops under cover of a white flag. Once he had permitted the burning of farms in these cases, officers in the field began applying the policy less judiciously, so that even before the occupation of Pretoria, widespread burning of homesteads was occurring.

Owing to continuing attacks on his rail and telegraphic communications, particularly in the Free State, from 16 June 1900 onwards, Roberts began burning down homesteads on farms in the immediate vicinity of each attack. In September 1900 he extended his policy to include the destruction or removal of all food and fodder supplies within a radius of 16 km, in order to cut the commandos off from their sources of supply. In practice this meant that an area of 547 km² was stripped for every attack or attempted attack on British lines of communication. Not surprisingly, British commanding officers in the field received the impression that they had Roberts' official approval to burn and destroy at will, and numerous homesteads went up in flames in areas where no attacks had been made.

In October 1900 Lieutenant-General Sir Archibald Hunter, operating in the northwestern Free State,

The concentration camps for Boer women and children evoked widespread condemnation of the British. French sympathies are evident in these scenes from *Le Petit Journal* (*right*) and from a postcard (*above*) showing the destruction of a Boer farm (Greenwall collection)

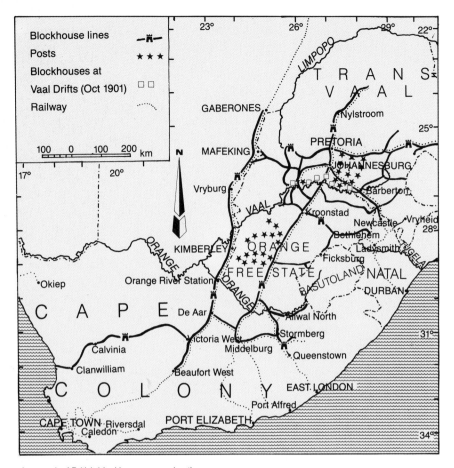

A network of British blockhouses spanning the country was part of Kitchener's plan to discourage the Boer commandos, while their families were removed to concentration camps and their farms were burned. The strategy succeeded in its objective

ordered the whole of Bothaville to be burned down, leaving only the government buildings, the church and the Red Cross depot. His grounds for this act were that Bothaville had served as a base for the commandos in their attacks on the railway lines.

Already in February 1900, and again in May and July of that year, the Boer leaders were protesting to Roberts about the burning of homesteads. The British commander-in-chief defended his policy by declaring that the war had largely degenerated into guerrilla warfare which he was forced to suppress 'by those exceptional methods which civilized nations have at all times found it obligatory to use under like circumstances'.[19]

In July 1900 Roberts sent some 2 500 Boer women and children to Boer lines in the eastern Transvaal, in an attempt to put pressure on the Boers through their women and children;

he hoped that their sufferings might persuade the Boers to lay down their arms. When this psychological manoeuvre failed, Roberts intensified his policy of destruction.

By November 1900 Roberts was experiencing growing resistance to his scorched earth policy, also in British government circles. As a result, on 18 November 1900 he issued orders to limit the burnings. According to Kitchener's calculations, as well as a British government publication, no more than 230 houses were burned down in November 1900. Even this was a gross underestimation, since Milner was to admit in October 1902 that as many as 30 000 houses had been destroyed during the war.[20] Few homesteads could have escaped destruction.

In the circumstances a major problem was obviously what to do with the growing number of homeless Boer women and children. In this way, the concentration camp system was ushered in. Precisely when the first camp was established is not known, but apparently by July 1900 a

camp for homeless women and children had been erected near Mafeking. At this stage the establishment of refugee camps was still not official policy.

The concentration camps

At this time Roberts was also obliged to protect Boers who had laid down their arms, to prevent them from being commandeered into further commando service. His solution was to place them and their families in protective refugee camps, two of which were erected – in Bloemfontein and Pretoria – in September 1900. However, from the outset these camps also contained homeless Boer women, children and old men who had not voluntarily sought British protection, the so-called 'undesirables' who soon outnumbered the refugees. In fact the name 'refugee camp' was a misnomer; the camps could only be called concentration camps. Before the end of 1900 other camps were established at Potchefstroom, Irene, Heidelberg, Heilbron, Kroonstad, Norvalspont, Pietermaritzburg and Port Elizabeth. Concentration camps for blacks, which will be discussed later, were also established.

On 29 November 1900 Kitchener took over supreme command in South Africa from Roberts. Despite his declared opposition to the scorched earth policy, Kitchener's command did not lead to any decrease in the burning down of homesteads. His instructions left the commanding officers in the field great leeway, and the burning of towns was continued – Wolmaransstad, Bethal, Ermelo, Carolina, Reitz, Parys and Lindley among them. Kitchener also continued the destruction of supplies with even greater determination than his predecessor. Crops were destroyed and cattle, sheep and horses slaughtered or driven to the British camps. Some animals were even mutilated and left to die in the veld. Kitchener, like Roberts, appears at times to have lost control over his subordinates' actions.

The claim that Kitchener was given the idea of concentration camps by Boers who had laid down their arms is unfounded. Kitchener simply organised more efficiently a system which had begun under Roberts. In the great drives launched by Kitch-

Above left British troops destroy a Boer farmhouse (Postcard, Greenwall collection)

Right A hardy group of Boer women obliged to surrender to the nearest British garrison because they no longer possessed draught animals (*Die Buren*)

Overleaf Two of Jean Veber's bitter cartoons condemning the concentration camps and Kitchener's bloody role. The same French cartoons were reissued as anti-British propaganda during World War I and II (*L'Assiette au Beurre*)

ener from January 1901 onwards, thousands of Boer women and children, the 'undesirables', were removed from their farms and placed in concentration camps – 'for humane reasons', Chamberlain announced in the House of Commons. But the fact that thousands of homesteads had been burned down and the women and children removed to the camps by force – as well as Kitchener's revelation that he insisted on different treatment for refugees who had laid down arms and for 'undesirables' – indicates that the camps were erected for military rather than humane reasons. They were plainly intended to undermine Boer resistance and persuade the burghers to lay down their arms in order to be reunited with their families.[21]

There is widespread testimony to the rough methods commanding officers in the field employed under the scorched earth policy. A British officer who witnessed the burning of a homestead noted: 'The women, in a little group, cling together, comforting each other or hiding their faces in each other's laps.'[22] A Boer woman declared: 'There I stood, surrounded by my small children, while the cruel soldiers plundered my property. Furniture, clothing, food, everything was thrown in a heap and set alight . . . Despite all my pleas that I might be allowed to retain a few antiques and heirlooms, they refused to listen.'[23]

The women and children were usually allowed to take with them a minimum of food, clothing and bedding. Often they were transported on open trucks or wagons, and in some instances they were made to walk long distances. Illness, physical disabilities and age were often ignored.

By September 1901 there were 34 concentration camps for whites in South Africa, with approximately 110 000 inmates, the majority of them children. The number did not increase drastically after this date, and after December 1901 few further civilians were sent to the camps.

In the camps, relations between women whose husbands were still on commando and those men who had surrendered were acrimonious. One woman went as far as to call such men 'the greatest pest in the camps', since they constantly reported resentful attitudes among the women to the camp authorities.

After the war Afrikaner bitterness towards British imperialism, as personified by Kitchener, centred largely around the high mortality rate in the concentration camps. *Methods of barbarism?*, a study of the camps by S. B. Spies, provides many useful insights. From the outset there were mortalities in the camps, but August to October 1901 represented a climax: in August 2 666 died (a death rate of 311 per 1 000 per year); in September 2 752 (287 per 1 000 per year) and in October 3 205 (344 per 1 000 per year). After the war P. L. A. Goldman officially determined that a shocking total of 27 927 Boers had died in the camps – 26 251 women and children (of whom over 22 000 were under the age of 16) and 1 676 males over 16 years, including 1 421 elderly.

There is no doubt that those interned in the concentration camps suffered miserably, as the following description from the camp at Brandfort shows: 'Among us was a Mrs Coetzee; she had eight children, but by now four had died. One day I passed her tent and saw three little boys lying on the ground on khaki blankets, with ants crawling all over them. The mother who had milk fever – her newborn son was already dead – was lying on a bedstead. Next to her lay a girl of seven years, also ill. To increase their misery, the tent was infested with lice. When necessary, the poor little boys had to get up without help, though their weak legs could hardly carry them.'[24]

The reasons behind the high mortality rate in the camps make appalling reading. In the first place, the war had inevitably brought unhygienic conditions in its wake and pollution of air, water and soil were sources of disease. Lowered standards of food production and unusually widespread outbreaks of measles and pneumonia claimed many casualties, especially among children.

A second reason for the high mor-

LES CAMPS DE RECONCENTRATION

..... Grâce à la bonne organisation des camps de reconcentration l'abondance et la santé y règnent. C'est un véritable plaisir de voir les enfants courir et jouer innocemment entre les tentes sous l'œil souriant de leurs mères qui oublient ainsi un moment la mélancolie de leur position.....

..... Les mesures de précaution que nous avons prises ont abaissé la mortalité des enfants à 380 pour mille.

(Rapport officiel au War office.)

... Je puis dire qu'à présent la guerre du Transvaal est terminée. Le pays est tranquille et j'y suis arrivé en évitant toute effusion de sang. Les camps de reconcentration où j'ai réuni les femmes et les enfants font rapidement leur œuvre de pacification...

(Rapport officiel du général Kitchener au War Office.)

tality rate in the camps must be sought in the unhygienic personal habits of the inmates. Medical men who visited the camps expressed this opinion, which Kitchener shared, and there was a measure of truth in their statements: some of the Boers in the camps were backward, undeveloped people whose ignorance and superstition, added to a refusal to undergo hospital treatment, contributed to their deaths. However, such attitudes were not the largest cause of the high mortality rate, as proved when the rate dropped considerably once the camps had been re-organised.

Poor camp administration emerges as the third and most important reason for the abnormal mortality rate. Several contributory factors may be isolated. Firstly, selection of some camp sites was unwise. At Standerton the soil became a soggy morass during the rainy season, while the winters were bitterly cold. Brandfort and Orange River were notorious for similar reasons.

Secondly, camp officials did not always maintain high standards of order and hygiene. In certain camps a shortage of adequate accommodation was reflected in the use of worn tents and even mud huts to shelter inmates, while others had to sleep on the ground when beds and mattresses were in short supply. Sanitation in the camps left much to be desired; and provision of water and firewood was inadequate.

A third factor was the poor quality of the food, particularly in the Transvaal camps. There was, however, a positive side: different standards for refugees and 'undesirables' were abolished in March 1901, and camp commanders were able to provide milk and other nourishing food for ill inmates and young children. Male internees were allowed to work and better their position by earning a little money, but most of the women's husbands were on commando, so that although from March 1901 internees were able to buy extra food at camp shops, poverty prevented most families from making use of this facility. Rebellious internees – and there were many of them – were not given a fair share of the food. Inmates did not always receive full rations, and the food itself was below standard.

The international storm of protest over the concentration camps was fuelled by eyewitness accounts from South Africa. The active concern of Englishwoman Emily Hobhouse (*above*) and reports by Cornelis Broeksma (*opposite, centre*) played their part. Broeksma, former public prosecutor of Johannesburg, was prominent in the church commission aiding the internees. Arrested and charged by the British authorities with breaking the oath of neutrality in smuggling his reports abroad, he was executed in September 1901

Emily Hobhouse arrived in South Africa in 1901 with a small fund for Boer women whose farms had been burned. As soon as she learned about the 'refugee' camps, she hastened to visit them and stayed to help, sending news of the appalling conditions she found in the earliest camps. Her criticism was heeded, but a separate committee was sent out to investigate and on her second visit Emily Hobhouse was forcibly restrained from landing in Cape Town

Rows of monotonous tents, supplemented by prefabricated huts less vulnerable to flooding, gave the concentration camps their regimented hopeless air, as seen in Brandfort camp (*opposite page, top*) and Harrismith camp (*right centre*), with the better sort of prefabricated house shown in a Natal camp (*bottom left*)

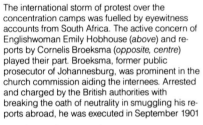

A group in Eshowe (*above right*), a camp established in 1902 in Natal, and the school in Standerton camp (*bottom right*) are indicative of improvements made by the end of the war (*Die Buren; After Pretoria*; postcards, Greenwall collection)

French interest in the Boer cause was strongly fuelled by anti-British sentiment. There were few surer ways to arouse sympathy for the Boers than to portray their women in idealistic terms – either as victims or as heroines

Above French postcards depicting the plight of Boer women as they are taken prisoner or attempt to protect their homes and children. The women and the interiors look more French than South African (Greenwall collection)

Opposite The sensationalist French weekly *Le Petit Parisien* ran this cover purporting to show Boer women joining their men in firing on the British. Despite the exaggeration and large artistic licence, there is a grain of truth, in that many Boer women were familiar with guns; some afterwards claimed to have fought in various battles. Certainly women were present in the Boer laagers and, given the flexibility of Boer military organisation, it is quite possible that some strong-willed women might have taken up arms. What is undoubtedly true is the Boer women were loyal republicans and an inspiration to their men in the field

Inadequate and inefficient medical staff had to cope with widespread disease. Resignations and dismissals between February 1901 and February 1902 led to the Transvaal camps losing 47 doctors of the original 94, plus 85 nurses out of 217, while 13 superintendents were replaced.

All these adverse factors stemmed from a basic weakness of organisation, for which S. B. Spies has rightly blamed Kitchener, since it was he who expanded the concentration camp system without due regard for its implications. Camp food supplies were eventually improved, and schools and properly staffed hospitals erected. The rapid influx of so many thousands of people, however, made efficient reform difficult, nor was there initially any pressure to improve camp conditions. Kitchener showed little interest in the administration of the camps: a soldier before all else, he gave military matters priority over civil issues.

An important factor working against efficient camp organisation was the official vagueness regarding precisely who was responsible for their administration. Under Roberts the few camps then in existence had been under military control. Although under Kitchener the camps were placed under civil administration as early as February 1901, they in fact remained under his indifferent supervision as army Commander-in-Chief until November 1901. Conditions worsened between May and August 1901, when Kitchener became Acting High Commissioner during Milner's visit to London. The success of Milner's efforts to improve camp conditions was evident after his return. During his absence the number of inmates in the concentration camps rose rapidly, but there was no corresponding increase

in the number of camps. In March 1901 there were 27 camps housing 35 000 whites. Six months later 110 000 whites overflowed a mere 34 camps.[25] Inevitably, as the number of internees increased, the mortality rate rose.

When the civil authorities assumed active control of the camps towards the middle of November 1901, a radical improvement occurred, with deaths dropping from 3 205 in October 1901 to 402 in March 1902, 298 in April and 196 in May of that year.[26]

The improvement had not, however, occurred by chance. It had been preceded by a long battle led by philanthropists – in particular Emily Hobhouse. As British coordinator of the South African Women and Children Distress Fund, she arrived in Cape Town in late December 1900 to gain first-hand information about local conditions. Here for the first time she learned about the network of concentration camps spread across the breadth of South Africa. Between January and April 1901 she visited the Free State camps, observing the distressing conditions and lending material assistance. Her sympathy and moral support earned her the great affection of the inmates.

On her return to England, Emily Hobhouse's revelations of the appalling suffering in the concentration camps fixed the attention of both government and opposition firmly on the military action that had been taken against innocent women and children. A storm of protest rose from the Liberal opposition in the severest outburst of criticism since the start of the war. The outcome of this was that the War Office appointed a commission of women under Millicent Fawcett to conduct an official investigation of conditions in the camps. Though Mrs Fawcett and one other member were both clearly unsympathetic towards the Boers, the commission was instrumental in bringing about significant reforms in the administration of the camps.

Before the report was completed in December 1901, the Fawcett commission made certain recommendations for improvements. These were put into practice with such speed and efficiency that the report was able to point to several improvements that had been made since the commis-

sion's visit to South Africa, including the appointment of roving inspectors, an increase in qualified doctors and nurses, and improved hospital accommodation. Milner and Chamberlain took the lead in ensuring the urgent improvements, since conditions in the camps and the unfavourable publicity the government was receiving were a source of grave concern to both.

S. B. Spies concludes that the concentration camp system established by Roberts and Kitchener may be regarded as a violation of the spirit of the Hague Convention, particularly with regard to Article 46: 'Family honour and rights, individual lives and private property . . . must be respected.'[27]

The National Women's Monument, designed by sculptor Anton van Wouw, was to be unveiled near Bloemfontein on 16 December 1913, to the memory of the women and children who died in the concentration camps during the Anglo-Boer War of 1899–1902.

Women in the veld

The scorched earth policy had claimed other victims: Boer women and their children who wandered in the veld for the entire duration of the war, or until they were herded into the concentration camps. Fear of the camps, and later the knowledge of the suffering and the high mortality rate they exacted, led many a family to prefer a harsh existence on the veld, even though they faced an unremitting struggle to evade the British columns. Women whose houses were burned down and who were not immediately taken to the camps certainly had no alternative but to remain homeless in the veld, often accompanied in their wanderings by loyal servants.

In mountainous regions in the eastern Free State and eastern Transvaal, the women and children took refuge in kloofs and caves. Visiting the deserted Swartruggens area in the western Transvaal in August 1900, Smuts was astonished to see them emerging 'like dassies' from the hills in the morning. If a house was still standing or had even one habitable room left, the family generally returned to it as soon as the British columns had passed. A Boer woman later related: 'We fled as many as six times with our stock and the furniture we were able to transport. We had to endure indescribable cold, discomfort and worry. When the enemy retreated a little and we were able to return to our homes we left our wagons ready loaded. More than once we thought we were safe until someone shouted: "The enemy is approaching!" and then what a hasty packing up, what shouting and moaning as we rounded up the oxen and so on. Women and young girls inspanned the oxen themselves and drove them, beating them with their bonnets and gloves or whatever they could lay hands on. I did it myself too – anything to avoid falling into the hands of the English!'

Since it was unsafe for women to remain on unprotected farms, families and friends combined to form laagers, which sometimes consisted of as many as 80 wagons plus numerous other vehicles. Certain laagers even had male commandants and the women themselves admitted that these laager commandants had their hands full keeping order. The laagers were seldom able to remain at a particular spot for any length of time for fear that Boer informers among the 'hands-uppers' might betray any such semi-permanent hiding place to the British.

In the final 18 months of the war fleeing laagers of women and children, as well as isolated families, frequently sought refuge in the neighbourhood of Boer commandos, occasionally even joining them. Jan Celliers noted in his diary: 'For the means of survival such poor families are dependent on passing commandos.' At other times Boer despatch riders and patrols, sometimes an entire commando, visited the women's laagers and were invited to share the women's meagre supplies of food.

During the war Boer women provided the fighting men with tremendous moral support. Four days before peace was concluded, Celliers noted: 'Nowhere do we meet a woman who doesn't encourage us to stand fast to the very end.'[28] In their turn, the men helped the women whenever they could, repairing damaged houses for them and frequently resisting British

patrols long enough to give the women and children a chance to escape. Since both the women and the Boer commandos generally moved about in their own districts in the last two years of the war, a burgher would often be briefly reunited with his family. For a little while life would seem almost normal.

On occasion women and children were caught in the crossfire between the Boers and the British, while in a few cases the British even fired on women when there was no commando in sight; some women and chil-

Opposite page Mrs Berrett, the Boer woman who claimed to have fought with her husband at Spionkop, photographed in ordinary dress and in her daring trouser outfit (*Heroes*)

Above, top Generals Louis Botha (*left*) and Lukas Meyer (*right*), with the wives who provided such loyal support. Rumour had it that Mrs Botha, who was descended from the family of the Irish patriot Robert Emmett, regularly passed on useful information from Pretoria to her husband in the field (*Cape Archives*)

Above The wife and children of General de Wet under guard in Johannesburg. General de la Rey's wife and children spent the war years travelling in a wagon (*After Pretoria*)

Mrs Eloff (*centre*) with her sisters, in a patriotic pose. She was the wife of Kruger's grandson and had preceded the President to Europe. There she formed part of his entourage as he travelled in search of support for the republican cause (Dutch postcard, Greenwall collection)

dren died or were wounded in this way.

For the women and children roaming the veld, obtaining provisions was a great problem, particularly once the scorched earth policy had devastated the farms. Their staple food was mealie pap, a porridge made from maize meal – in this case usually of necessity without salt. Many women cultivated small patches of wheat in isolated spots. A burgher remarked: 'It is sad to see women and girls working in the fields and leading water. But this is the spirit that has withstood the Khakis for three years, the spirit they have not been able to crush.'[29] A number of women obtained permission from the first Brit-

ish officers they met to keep their cows for the younger children's milk – only to have the cows taken from them by later columns.

In their writings some Boer women made it clear that they had been treated discourteously and even cruelly by the British. But there were also many instances of humane treatment which the women recorded with gratitude.

Illness was a serious problem for the wandering families, since they were unable to procure any medicines; simple Boer remedies were all the women had to treat even the most serious of diseases. One woman later related that most of them had suffered periodic attacks of fever, while another claimed: 'In such times you learn to know your Saviour well and you come to rely on Him alone.'[30]

Increasing black hostility posed a further threat to the homeless women and children, with armed blacks roaming the countryside in groups, plundering and looting. The murders in the predominantly male laagers at Derdepoort (November 1899) and Holkrantz (May 1902) caused grave concern in the female laagers too. There were isolated incidents of assault and rape of Boer women during the war.

In the final six months of the war, when the British were no longer sending women and children to the concentration camps, the sufferings of the women in the veld increased greatly, owing to the by then almost complete devastation of the land. In addition, the extensive network of blockhouses severely limited the women's movements. Jan Celliers describes how their courage, dedication, patience and unremitting support earned them the admiration of the burghers on commando. 'To see the women in torn dresses and some in rags and tatters, was for us the bitterest part of the war,' said General Ben Viljoen.[31] Though there were some women who lost courage and tried to persuade the men to surrender, most women's suffering in the veld simply hardened their resolution.

Probably the best known Boer woman who constantly evaded the British was Nonnie de la Rey, wife of the renowned Boer general. With a heavily loaded wagon and a two-

wheeled spider, she roamed the western Transvaal for the last 19 months of the war, accompanied by her children, three servants and a motley crew of cows, sheep and chickens. The small company had several narrow escapes from the concentration camps. Somehow the general always knew where to find his family and visited them whenever he could. Mrs de la Rey later recorded her experiences, translated as *A woman's wanderings and trials during the Anglo-Boer War*.

At the peace conference at Vereeniging in May 1902, General Botha informed the delegates that there were some 2 540 Boer families still wandering about the Transvaal, cared for by the commandos whenever possible. This amounted to about 10 000 women and children. There were fewer in the Free State, though some of the Free State delegates reported at Vereeniging that their districts were practically depopulated. Others emphasised the great liability the wandering families had represented for the commandos, particularly in the districts of Winburg, Ladybrand and Heilbron.

The suffering of the women and children, both in the camps and in the veld, merely made many bitter enders more determined to continue the struggle. But eventually a turning point was reached, and the Boer representatives at Vereeniging expressed the feeling that the women and children could not be allowed to suffer further. Combined with other important considerations – the devastation caused by the scorched earth policy, the fact that the British had begun arming blacks who were hostile to the Boers, and the desperately unequal nature of the battle against a superior British force – the suffering of the Boer women and children was a powerfully persuasive argument for peace.

With the winter of 1902 looming, peace was finally concluded. Martha Kriel from the Ladybrand district summed up the feelings of the women in the veld when she said: 'Through all the dangers and oppression, we have always cherished the hope that we would regain our freedom. Our dear Lord has decided otherwise, and we must be content.'[32]

CHAPTER 7

Hensoppers and joiners

For years after the Anglo-Boer War the actions of the hensoppers (literally hands uppers, those Boers who surrendered) and the joiners (Boers who crossed to the British forces) caused a deep rift in Afrikanerdom. They were regarded as traitors to the national cause and were constantly compared, to their great discredit, with the bitter enders who remained loyal to the end. After nearly a century, the motives of the hensoppers and joiners can be examined more objectively. Since the republics were not defeated until 31 May 1902, the actions of the hensoppers and joiners were unavoidably treasonable.

The Boers who laid down their arms, the so-called hensoppers, were chiefly burghers who started out fighting on the Boer side but later voluntarily surrendered their arms to the British military authorities. Usually, they took the oath of neutrality at the same time. The joiners, significantly, went a step further. Initially hensoppers themselves, they fought actively on the British side against the Boers.

The surrender of Cronje with 4 000 men on 27 February 1900, and the fall of Bloemfontein two weeks later, led to widespread dejection among the burghers and was one of the reasons many Boers surrendered. De Wet

Boer punishment of traitors, illustrated with lurid effect in *Le Petit Parisien*

gave the Free Staters leave of absence until 25 March 1900, and while large numbers of the burghers rejoined their commandos, others lost heart at this stage and surrendered their arms. De Wet correctly attributed the general despair to Roberts' proclamations, which had been issued from February 1900.

In these 'paper bombs', as the Boers called them, particularly the proclamation of 15 March, Roberts encouraged the burghers to lay down their arms, assuring them that if they took an oath not to participate in any further warfare they would be allowed to return to their homes. They would not be taken as prisoners of war, nor would their property be confiscated. After the occupation of Pretoria on 5 June 1900, Roberts repeated his offer in the ZAR. In addition he annexed the Free State and the ZAR as British territories, on 24 May and 1 September 1900 respectively.

The irresolution of some of the burghers may also be attributed to poor discipline in the early phase of the war, and to the organisation of the commandos. The burghers were un-used to protracted military service, and there was little to hold those who grew weary of the fighting and wished to lay down their arms to return to their families or resume their farming.

A. M. Grundlingh distinguishes three specific types of motivation to surrender among the Boers. Some were convinced that continuing the struggle was unrealistic and a danger to their country – in their opinion a swift end to the war was in Boer interests. Others simply grew tired of fighting and no longer cared about the outcome of the struggle. Then there was the self-interest of certain Boers who put their personal welfare first and wished to see the end of hostilities so that their property would no longer be exposed to destruction.[33]

Although Roberts was soon compelled to admit that the war was by no means over, his victories and the accompanying proclamations did serve to weaken Boer resistance. In the Free State some 6 000 burghers availed themselves of his offer and surrendered between March and July 1900.

This figure does not include burghers who were forced to surrender and were sent to prisoner of war camps, such as the 4 400 burghers who surrendered under Prinsloo. Before the end of June 1900 nearly 8 000 Transvalers voluntarily laid down their arms. The period between March and July 1900 thus also represents the phase during which Boers began collaborating with the British.

Refugee camps were erected in the latter half of 1900 for those who had laid down their arms, in order to prevent their being molested by fighting Boers or being pressed into commando service again. Most burghers surrendering between January 1901 and the end of the war were placed in these camps, which they shared with the women and children of Boers who were still fighting. The hensoppers' hostile attitude to these women and children, and the contempt the women in turn expressed towards the hensoppers, led to extremely bitter relations between the two groups, not least because the hensoppers generally enjoyed preferential treatment in the camps.

Some of the families of the hensoppers fled to neighbouring states with their stock; after the war these assets enabled them to recover financially far sooner than their compatriots. Hensoppers who remained in the republics tried from time to time to persuade the burghers still on commando to surrender. This paved the way for the formation of the Burgher Peace Committees, which enjoyed the support of the British authorities.

In December 1900 Kitchener approved the establishment of a central Burgher Peace Committee in Pretoria, from which local committees in the Transvaal and Free State sprang. Their message to the burghers on commando was that further resistance was fruitless and that the republics could not rely on intervention by foreign powers. Ironically, the chairman of the central committee in the Free State was the brother of Christiaan de Wet, General Piet de Wet, who had surrendered in July 1900.

Early in 1901 the Burgher Peace Committees began visiting Boers on commando to urge them to lay down their arms. They also distributed circulars discussing peace negotiations. In January 1901, a few months before his death, the ageing ex-president M. W. Pretorius visited Louis Botha in an attempt to persuade him to conclude peace.

Such peace-makers invariably met with a cool reception, some being fined or arrested, while Meyer de Kock was found guilty of high treason and died before a Boer firing squad. Among the ordinary burghers, however, pleas for peace met with more success and the number of burghers voluntarily surrendering their arms rose steadily in February and March 1901.

Under Piet de Wet's leadership, a peace delegation travelled to the Cape Colony to visit local political leaders and churchmen among the Afrikaners, and the prisoners of war at Green Point. Their only gain was the establishment of a separate camp for those prisoners of war who were in favour of peace.

After the emergence of the peace committees, the next logical step appeared to be nothing less than active collaboration with the British military authorities. A clear polarisation

Opposite page 'Boers taking the oath of neutrality at Greylingstad', drawn by H. M. Paget from a sketch by Lt E. Blake Knox (*Buller's Campaign*)

Boers who surrendered to the British were disarmed and allowed to return to their farms. However, since they faced only burnt out ruins and possible retribution from Boers still fighting, some chose to join the better camps as refugees, like these surrendered Boers at Standerton (*above*), working in a quarry for much needed remuneration (*After Pretoria*)

Right Piet de Wet, brother of General Christiaan de Wet, was one of the major forces behind peace moves during the guerrilla stage of the war. He took up arms against the Boers as leader of the Heilbron section of the Orange River Colony Volunteers (*After Pretoria*)

Overleaf The flogging of Morgendaal, one of Piet de Wet's peace envoys, by Commandant Froneman. General de Wet, shown watching behind the beaten man, was himself notoriously free with the sjambok. The outcome of this incident was that Morgendaal was shot by Froneman on de Wet's orders. Ten days later he died of his wounds. Wash drawing by F. Waugh (Greenwall collection)

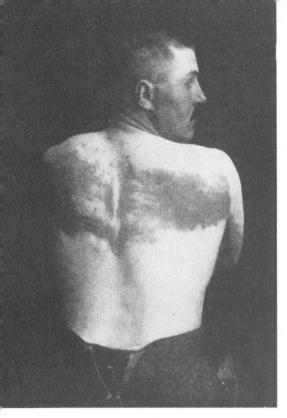

A rough reply for another Boer pleading peace – a rebel who surrendered and returned to persuade his brother to do the same. He was beaten with wet stirrup leathers (*After Pretoria*)

emerged in the Boer ranks, dividing those who regarded continued resistance as futile and destructive, and those who clung to their cause and were determined to continue fighting for their independence.

When the Boer leaders refused to be swayed by their arguments, certain peace-makers resorted to more drastic action. By late September 1901 the central peace committee of the Free State had decided to raise a burgher corps to assist the British columns in the field. The establishment of the National Scouts and the Orange River Colony Volunteers was a direct result of the failure of the peace movement among the Boers.

A. M. Grundlingh points to an important economic motive behind many hensoppers' decision to become joiners. The great majority of joiners were members of an underprivileged class. Before the war, they had either drifted to towns or eked a meagre living on farms as bywoners (landless families). Consequently even before the war they had formed a dissatisfied and dispossessed group who were easily swayed by vague British promises of a more privileged

position after the war. In addition, the British military authorities paid them for their services in the field, whereas in the commandos they had fought without remuneration. However, economic pressure did not prevent there being many bywoners among the bitter enders.

Family ties, always important among Afrikaners, may have led certain burghers to support the British war effort simply because an influential member of their family had done so, and it was common to find a father and his sons, as well as sons-in-law, brothers and cousins, all joining the National Scouts.

Others joined the National Scouts simply to escape the appalling conditions in the concentration camps, while leaders such as Piet de Wet, ex-Commandant S. G. Vilonel of the Free State, and ex-General A. P. J. Cronjé of the Transvaal (brother of General Piet Cronjé) believed that they could hasten the advent of peace by taking up arms on the British side.

Joiners saw active service on the British side as guides and scouts, as National Scouts and Orange River Colony Volunteers, and in the local burgher corps. The first burgher corps was established in the Free State in November 1900. The corps, like the guides and scouts, were employed by the British on a casual basis and were not bound by official conditions of service; they neither received British uniforms, nor were sworn in as soldiers of the British Army. Compensation was either financial or in the form of a share in whatever livestock they looted.

With the exception of the Farmer's Guard in the Bloemfontein district, which had 615 men in its employ by the end of the war, the local burgher corps remained small. The British did not make extensive use of them, beyond their basic task of claiming livestock from the farms of burghers on commando, or acting as guides for the British columns. The corps were in fact little more than freebooters, and as such they were moderately successful. During 1901 a burgher corps under Captain O. M. Bergh, consisting of Boers who had surrendered and a certain number of blacks, attacked Boer forces in the vicinity of Winburg. There is evidence that they

also burned down homesteads and molested women and children.

The British began using joiners as guides as early as June 1900. In the last 18 months of the war the practice increased sharply until by April 1902 all British columns had joiner guides. They were generally drawn from the concentration camps, though others had offered their services voluntarily as soon as they were taken prisoners of war. The guides were usually employed for as long as the British column operated in an area familiar to them.

With their knowledge of the terrain and of the Boers' military tactics, these guides filled a crucial gap in the British army, particularly in the successful nocturnal attacks launched by British columns on the Transvaal Highveld and in the Free State from the winter of 1901. Eleven joiners were acting as guides for Brigadier-General R. G. Broadwood's column when it took several key figures of the Free State government prisoner at Reitz on 11 July 1901. Confidential official documents were captured and President Steyn barely escaped being taken prisoner on this occasion.

Sometimes joiner guides led British columns to the farms of Boers who were away on active service; the homesteads were burned and the women and children removed to concentration camps. The anger and contempt of the bitter enders and their wives was such that guides who fell into Boer hands generally received the death penalty.

Joiners also rendered valuable service to the British military intelligence as scouts operating from British lookout posts and as such were chiefly involved in tracing and capturing small groups of burghers in the field.

In October 1901 Kitchener approved a scheme to utilise the military contribution of the burgher corps and the guides more efficiently. The largest burgher corps, the National Scouts, was extended and officially incorporated into the British army. Kitchener not only regarded the joiners as a great asset to the British forces, but also hoped to increase the existing division amongst the Afrikaners, to Britain's advantage. All members of the re-organised National Scouts were required to take the oath of allegiance to the British Crown. Unlike the members of the local burgher corps, they were formally sworn in as soldiers of the British army.

From October 1901, with the help of former Boer officers such as A. P. J. Cronjé, the British authorities canvassed members for the National Scouts, particularly in the Transvaal concentration camps. Attractive conditions were offered, including a half share of confiscated livestock and 2s 6d a day; the amount was increased to 5s a day in January 1902. But many promises made in the couse of canvassing for the National Scouts were hollow and could not have been honoured with the best will in the world.

Besides the men canvassed in the concentration camps, many Boers joining the Scouts had been newly taken prisoner in the field. Again, the willingness of these burghers to collaborate with the British stemmed from a growing conviction that the Boer struggle was doomed and that only drastic measures would bring the burghers who were still fighting to their senses.

The National Scouts were now provided with a full military khaki uniform, as well as a horse, saddle, bridle, rifle and ammunition. The local burgher corps, on the other hand, received only rifles and ammunition and were expected to provide the rest of their equipment themselves. Though the commandants of the National Scouts were in charge of their columns, they were subordinate to Major E. M. H. Leggett and his officers. Each column, consisting of some 50 Scouts, was also under the supervision of a British lieutenant.

The families of many of the National Scouts were allowed to occupy houses in the towns, while the wives and children of bitter enders were forced to remain in their tents in the concentration camps. In December 1901 the authorities decided to erect separate camps for the families of Scouts; although they received no more food than the internees of other concentration camps, they did enjoy greater freedom of movement and excellent medical facilities.

The Orange River Colony Volunteers, established in March 1902, were the brother corps of the Transvaal National Scouts in the Free State and operated under the same conditions of service. The efforts of Piet de Wet and S. G. Vilonel were largely responsible for the formation of the ORC Volunteers. In joining the National Scouts and the ORC Volunteers, some of the burghers who had surrendered thus took a radical step further by formally taking up arms against their fellow burghers.

None of the various sections of the National Scouts ever went into action as a separate task force against the Boers, but instead did useful work as guide or scout corps attached to the British columns. A total of 1 359 Scouts, from nine sections, were readily accepted by the British officers and troops and participated in a number of encounters with the Boers, as at Yzerspruit on 25 February 1902, Tweebosch on 7 March 1902 and Roodewal on 11 April 1902. The presence of the Scouts did not however have any decisive effect on these battles. They were only prepared to attack if they were in a more favourable position than the Boers.

In the Free State the ORC Volunteers were not involved in any clashes with the Boers; their participation in the war was restricted to the role of scouts and guides for the British columns. One section, comprising 248 men, was stationed at Heilbron under Piet de Wet; the other, consisting of 200 men, was under Vilonel at Winburg.

The activities of the National Scouts and the ORC Volunteers naturally evoked great bitterness among the Boers who were still on commando, strengthening the resolve of many of the fighting burghers to continue the struggle. But on others the activities had a demoralising effect, and cannot be ignored as a factor in the eventual move towards peace. The fact is that an increasing number of burghers who had surrendered were willing to collaborate with the British war effort. British statistics indicate that by the middle of January 1902 the joiners numbered 1 660, by February 2 500, by the end of April 3 963 and on 1 June 1902, the day after peace was concluded, as many as 5 464. The vast majority were guides or scouts attached to British columns. The figures for the National Scouts alone were 950 at the start of January 1902, 1 125 by April and 1 359 by the end of the war. By the end of April 1902, the ORC Volunteers numbered 385, rising to 448 by the conclusion of peace.[34]

The increasing split between the 'bittereinders' and the Boers who surrendered is underlined in this drawing of Boers eager to join the National Scouts after a speech by Kitchener. Drawn by F. de Harnen from a photograph (*Transvaal War*)

CHAPTER 8

Blacks and the war

Although the Anglo-Boer War of 1899-1902 was mainly a war between the British and the Boers, it also unavoidably affected other population groups in South Africa. Moreover, coloureds and, more particularly, blacks were involved in the war in both active and non-combatant roles.

The two Boer republics each had a black majority within their borders. Figures given by Ram and Thomson, Netherlands military attachés with the Boers, indicate that there were 289 000 whites and 755 000 blacks resident in the ZAR, and 78 000 whites as against 130 000 blacks in the Free State.

The political and economic situation of the blacks on the eve of the war merits attention. During the 19th century the black tribes had gradually fallen under white control. Britain annexed Basutoland (Lesotho) in 1868 and in 1885 extended a protectorate over Bechuanaland (Botswana). Zululand was incorporated into Natal in 1897. With the Swaziland Conventions of 1890 and 1894, the administration of Swaziland was entrusted to the ZAR. In the ZAR itself the Pedi chief Sekhukhune was subjugated in 1879, and the Venda under Mphephu in 1898.

Left A captured spy struggles against his fate (*War with the Boers*)

Inset above Black scout with Montmorency's Scouts. Sketch by A. McNeill (Greenwall)

Top right Blacks, probably mine workers, leave by train after the relief of Kimberley (*War Impressions*)

During these years the black population groups also surrendered their economic independence. Large areas were taken over for white settlement. A system of migrant labour emerged in which the whites became dependent on black labour, and the blacks in turn dependent on the economy and industries of the whites.

There was an unspoken agreement between the leaders of the Boers and the British that this was 'a white man's war' and that the blacks should not be armed for the struggle. The whites of South Africa, a small minority group outnumbered by the black population in their midst, saw no reason to give blacks the deciding voice in an issue they regarded as their exclusive concern. As Ram and Thomson remarked in their war report: 'The use of black soldiers is condemned from a political point of view; the Boer is strongly of the opinion that the black man is an inferior being; to regard him as the white man's equal is abhorrent to the Boer.'[35]

The official British opinion was that it would be 'bad policy' to arm blacks for the struggle. Britain was not prepared to offend the whites in the Cape Colony and Natal unnecessarily, nor did she wish to pave the way

for a social revolution in South Africa.

In his useful study on the subject. *Black people and the South African War 1899-1902*, Peter Warwick points out that large numbers of blacks supported the British war effort politically as well as militarily, pinning their hopes on a British victory. There was an elite among coloureds, Indians and black groups who believed that Britain would promote their cause in the event of victory. Past British actions and certain pre-war declarations by Britain led them to hope for an extension of Cape voting qualifications to the north.

The Indians in South Africa came down overwhelmingly on Britain's side. At the beginning of the war, even though he regarded the Boer cause as just, the influential Mohandas Gandhi called upon his fellow countrymen to support the British in order to prove their loyalty to the Crown and safeguard their freedom as members of the British Empire. During the war the role of South African Indians was on the whole limited to stretcher-bearing after battles on the Natal front, a duty Gandhi himself undertook after the Battle of Spionkop. In Natal in particular, Indians

also proved useful as war-time shopkeepers.

In Swaziland the Dlamini clan hoped that a Boer defeat would strengthen their own dominance in the Swazi community. Similarly, the Sekhukune supporters among the Pedi engaged in military collaboration with the British army in order to regain their former influence over Pedi affairs and to extend their territory. Other black groups in the ZAR entered the service of the British war effort with much the same motive, particularly after the fall of the republican capitals. In addition, sheer poverty made thousands of black labourers available to the British.

Interestingly enough, both the British and the Boer military authorities armed friendly black tribes at the start of the war – with the sole aim of protecting their territories' borders, rather than to set black against white. Both sides thus ensured security on their own fronts and at the same time freed more units for action elsewhere. The ZAR armed blacks who were living along the Crocodile River in the Waterberg district in November 1899, as well as others near Dundee in Natal. The British armed several of the black tribes along the republican

borders: in Bechuanaland the Kgatla under Lentshwe, and between 800 and 1 000 Ngwato under Kgama; 4 000 Mfengu and Thembu in the Transkei; and 500 Rolong in Mafeking. Armed coloureds and blacks in the Cape Colony periodically accompanied British columns sent out to halt Boer advances.

The arming of the Kgatla had unfortunate consequences in the Marico district of the ZAR. Three Kgatla regiments under Lentshwe's half-brother Segale attacked a Boer laager at Derdepoort on 25 November 1899. They were acting on the orders of Colonel G.S. Holdsworth and were covered by his division. Holdsworth's force soon fell back, while the Kgatla continued the attack. Boer sources indicate that six burghers died, among them Jan Barnard, the local Volksraad representative. Kgatla figures however indicate that between 25 and 35 burghers lost their lives. At least 15 Kgatla died in the attack, while 17 were wounded. The Kgatla also attacked the white settlement 1 km from the laager. Two white women were killed and 17 white women and children were abducted to Bechuanaland. Many Boer families, fearing further attacks, formed laagers or fled to Rustenburg for safety.

From the start of the war British and Boer forces alike had employed blacks in non-combatant roles. In the British army they were particularly employed as wagon drivers, with an estimated minimum of 14 000 such drivers in employ at any given time during the war. Blacks were also hired to build the British blockhouses and employed in sanitation and other menial labour in the military camps, such as minding the horses and slaughter stock, or offloading supplies.

According to Warwick, other forms of black labour in the British army cannot so easily be regarded as non-combatant services. Some blacks certainly acted as scouting and intelligence aides. In Natal the Zululand Native Scouts were an established

Top left Martial law in the Cape Colony obliged all citizens, including blacks, to hand in their guns (Cape Archives)

Left, below Roadmender in the service of the Royal Engineers (*After Pretoria*)

Everywhere blacks were deeply affected by the war. Refugees from the Transvaal included these Indians (*top left*) photographed in camp in Cape Town (*Transvaal War*); while in Natal, with its large Indian population, many served as ambulance dhoolie bearers (*below*), carrying the wounded from the battlefield on stretchers. A young lawyer named Mohandas Gandhi was the organiser of these ambulance teams and himself carried wounded from the battle of Spionkop (*After Pretoria*)

Above right Charles Sheldon's drawing shows a court of summary jurisdiction in action during the siege of Mafeking. In this case the prisoners on trial are extremely young, and were probably caught stealing food, an offence strictly punished on Baden-Powell's orders. The interpreter in the centre is the black journalist Sol Plaatje (*War with the Boers*)

force, while coloured scouting groups were founded in the northern and northwestern Cape. Black scouts were extremely useful to the British during the guerrilla phase of the war when smaller, more mobile columns scoured the veld in search of scattered Boer commandos. Black scouts corps of up to 50 men under the command of a white officer were attached to all British columns; one of the most successful of these black corps in the guerrilla phase was led by Colonel A. Woolls-Sampson.

Certain categories of service in the British army proved very lucrative for blacks. Good drivers and scouts could earn up to 90s a month, against an average monthly wage for other services of 40-50s. Food was included, and clothing and blankets were occasionally issued.

During the guerrilla phase of the war, the ZAR to a great extent lost control over the black tribes within its borders. Boer families and officials were driven out of large areas of the western Transvaal (particularly the Marico district) and from the eastern Transvaal between the Olifants and Steelpoort Rivers, paving the way for further black participation on the

This Dutch postcard lampoons the British for sending Kgatla regiments ahead of Holdsworth's column, during the attack on the Boers at Derdepoort in November 1899 (Greenwall)

British side. Black tribesmen raided many Boer farms and drove plundered livestock to the British garrisons, where they received a share of the booty. Blacks also took part in the transportation of Boer women and children to the concentration camps.

Several black tribes collaborated with the British army by denying Boer commandos access to their territories. The Boers, already pinned against blockhouse lines by Kitchener's drives, found their freedom of movement further curtailed, while on the British side more columns were freed for service in the field.

During the first year of the war, at the request of the British government, Roberts issued strict orders that blacks were on no account to be armed for active service against the Boers. Even blacks employed by the British army were threatened with severe punishment if they donned military uniform.

Kitchener's attitude to the use of blacks in the war was far more flexible than Roberts' had been. When he assumed command towards the end of 1900, there had already been suggestions that blacks employed by the British army should be armed for the purpose of self-defence against the Boers, who had begun executing black scouts falling into their hands. Moreover, the British army's manpower was on the wane.

In December 1900 it was decided that black scouts who possessed arms at employment would no longer be disarmed. Seven months later, in July 1901, matters took an important turn when General P. H. Kritzinger in the Cape Colony warned Kitchener that blacks or coloureds employed by the British army would be executed if caught by the Boers, whether they

were armed or not. Both the British army and the British government consequently decided there was no further need to prevent black scouts from carrying arms for self defence. During the latter half of 1901 most black scouts attached to British columns in the Transvaal and Free State were issued with arms.

This concession opened the way for the arming of other categories of blacks engaged in British military service. Owing to the British shortage of manpower, blacks were armed to guard the blockhouses and blockhouse lines. Severe criticism of this policy came in particular from the Liberal opposition in Britain. Kitchener evaded the War Office's periodic questions regarding the number of armed blacks in the British army, until mounting pressure forced him to supply figures in March 1902: there were 2 496 blacks and 2 939 coloureds in the Cape, and 4 618 blacks in Natal, the Free State and the Transvaal – a total of 10 053.[36]

Kitchener's figures do not however represent the total number of armed blacks in British military service in South Africa. Many blacks, especially among the scouts, had provided their own arms – a practice that was permitted after December 1900. In March 1902 Lloyd George asserted in the House of Commons that there were as many as 30 000 armed blacks in British service in South Africa. If his figure is accurate, and Warwick does not regard it as greatly exaggerated, this means that at the conclusion of the war armed blacks on the British side outnumbered the Boer bitter enders on commando by 50 per cent. Even if the figure was in fact closer to 20 000, it would still have equalled the number of bitter enders.

The Boers made no provision for blacks in their active military ranks, but like the British they did employ friendly blacks in non-combatant capacities, to strengthen their war attempt. In the ZAR, Act 20 of 1898 and Act 21 of 28 September 1899 made provision for this, with the former act allowing blacks to be called upon for personal duty, or to contribute to war costs or work on the farms of burghers who were on active service. The Free State had similar legislation.

Service for blacks on the Boer side

involved in digging trenches, often alongside the burghers, plus wagon driving and other heavy labour. They were also used by the Boers as scouts, but to a lesser degree and usually without their being armed, as they increasingly were on the British side.

Despite republican policy, in a few cases blacks on the Boer side did take up arms. During the siege of Mafeking, General J.P. Snyman armed local Tswana in February 1900 'for security reasons'. When the ZAR government learned of this, the Tswana were disarmed and dismissed. In Natal, black labourers who absconded to the British camps from Boer laagers repeatedly claimed that armed blacks were accompanying the commandos. The commandos around Ladysmith were also reported to be using armed blacks for night sentry duty. In many such cases, however, the blacks may have been agterryers (literally after riders) carrying their masters' bandoliers and rifles.

At the outbreak of hostilities many farmers took their best labourers on commando as their agterryers. In many cases these were men who had been in the service of the Boer family for years, often growing up with their masters on the farm. The relationship between a burgher and his agterryer was usually one of friendly understanding, based on a paternalism which the agterryer appeared to accept.

The agterryer's task was to ride out behind his employer, bringing a spare mount or the pack-horses. During halts agterryers guarded the horses, fetched water and firewood, built the fires and frequently did the cooking. When the Boers rode out to battle, the agterryers and a few burghers would stay at a safe distance with the pack-horses.

The most valued agterryers were generally those who had been in their employers' service the longest and who identified themselves with the Boer cause. In his memoirs General Ben Bouwer recalled: 'Some of them were tenacious fellows and clung to their masters long after the master would have been glad to be relieved of the responsibility, and when they themselves could have found much easier living by changing to the other side.'[37]

Although the Boers did not regard their agterryers as their equals, their memoirs, diaries and letters while on commando reveal that the agterryer was invariably more than a servant. They reportedly remained cheerful even under the trying conditions of the final guerrilla years, adopting the burghers' songs and sports as their own.

Humour was never absent among the agterryers. One jocularly said that when the Boers were forced to retreat, he himself never delayed retiring 'because I always thought if they (the English) caught me, I would have to speak to them, but how could I if I did not even have one word of English?'[38]

The best known case of an agterryer saving his master's life and possessions is the story of Ruiter, President Steyn's young agterrryer. When the laager of the Free State government was surprised by the British at Reitz, in July 1901, Ruiter not only warned Steyn in time for him to escape on his horse, but misled the British into believing that the distant rider they saw was 'just an old Boer'. Ruiter then led the British officer a merry dance in search of the President, who had long since escaped to safety.

Sources reveal that some agterryers resented the ban on their bearing arms, and on occasion acquired arms illegally. Desertion by agterryers was a further problem which began occurring before the British occupation of Kroonstad in May 1900. By mid September 1900 an agterryer was a rare luxury among the burghers of the Pretoria commando, which operated under Commandant C. P. S. Badenhorst along the Croco-dile River. Agterryers who deserted sometimes joined the British columns, taking with them their intimate knowledge of the Boer laagers.

Since the agterryers were not counted as part of the Boer fighting force, there is no official record of their numbers. However, the diaries and other informal Boer sources reveal that friends and relatives frequently shared the service of a single agterryer, so that an estimate of some 10 000 agterryers does not appear to be unreasonable.

The ordeal of the concentration camp was not restricted to Boer women and children. Thousands of black men, women and children underwent similar trials. By July 1900 many

A Boer and his agterryer, who brought up his spare mount and equipment, and prepared his meals. Agterryers were usually trusted servants from the Boers' own farms (Denis Godfrey collection)

blacks, mostly the women and children, had begun fleeing their tribal areas to seek protection from the British authorities. When Kitchener issued orders on 21 December 1900 that all districts were to be cleared of inhabitants, he ruled that his columns were to bring in only those blacks who were living on Boer farms.

At the start of Kitchener's intensive drives in January 1901, particularly those in the eastern Transvaal, blacks were removed not only from Boer farms but from their kraals and even from mission stations. Already in March 1901 there were complaints by blacks that British troops were setting their huts on fire; by October 1901 the burning of kraals by British columns was standard practice.

The removal of blacks from the theatre of war to the camps was initially devoid of humanitarian considerations. Kitchener's aim was to prevent Boer commandos from obtaining any type of assistance from blacks. He had also from the outset intended to draw on black male labour for his war effort.[40]

When a black family was brought into a British garrison, the able-bodied men were assigned to the nearest military department as labourers, usually for a three month period after which they were allowed to return to their families for a time. The labourers received rations plus a shilling a day, enabling them to support their families in camps erected alongside the white concentration camps. Separate camps for blacks and whites was the general rule, although in some cases servants were allowed to work for former employers who had been placed in the concentration camps, while blacks were also employed for sanitary and other tasks in the white camps.

During the first six months of 1901, a number of totally independent concentration camps were established for blacks. By July 1901 there were nearly 38 000 blacks in the camps, over 30 000 of them women and children. They were sent to the concentration camps right up to the end of the war, so that numbers in their camps increased steadily, while the white camps gradually declined in population. By May 1902 no fewer than 29 black camps fell under the control of the Free State administration, plus 37 camps in the Transvaal – a total of 115 000 inmates.[41]

In the Transvaal black concentration camps were situated, among others, at Heidelberg Standerton, Nigel, Potchefstroom, Middelburg and Nelspruit. Free State camps included Heilbron, Winburg, Harrismith, Thaba Nchu and Kimberley.

No particular distinction appears to have been made between different tribes – in certain cases Zulu and Mfengu inmates protested against being placed in the same camps.

During the first half of 1901, black concentration camps were controlled by the superintendents of the white camps, but in June that year the Native Refugee Department took over the administration of black camps in the Transvaal. The Department was headed by a Canadian, Major G. de Lotbinière, whose responsibility was extended to black camps in the Free State on 1 August 1901.

Two major reasons lay behind the creation of the Refugee Department. One was the realisation that only a separate department would be able to counteract long-standing neglect of the black camps. More importantly, a full-time department was required to recruit labourers in the camps. The aim was to replace those miners who were engaged in military service for the British, thus releasing them to return to the Witwatersrand goldmines. The Native Refugee Department was extremely successful in supplying labour for the British army: by the end of 1901 over 6 000 blacks had been recruited for the army, and the figure rose to over 13 000 by April 1902. Black men, women and children were also placed in the service of private employers in the vicinity of the camps.

Self-sufficiency was the rule in the black camps, where inmates were required to erect their own accommodation. In August 1901 Kitchener approved a scheme to allow inmates to cultivate crops for their own consumption, not only as an economy measure but in the hope of attracting more blacks to the camps as a vital source of labour for the army.

Large areas were set aside for cultivation, and the camps were moved closer to the railway lines; here the inmates would in addition be safer. Deserted farms were frequently also utilised for cultivation, which was a task left to the women and children and those men unfit for army labour. Potatoes, pumpkins and fodder crops were produced to supplement British army supplies, while maize and sorghum were grown for black consumption.

Before the harvest, needy blacks in the camps were able to draw free rations of mealie meal. Those who were employed bought their mealie meal, besides such war-time luxuries as sorghum, sugar, coffee, tea, syrup and tobacco. Salt was on free issue, while milk was provided at the recommendation of the doctors who periodically visited the camps.

As in the white concentration camps, the mortality rate in the black camps rose alarmingly in the latter half of 1901, but whereas mortality in the white camps fell after October 1901, half of the deaths in the black camps occurred in the three months between November 1901 and January 1902 alone. December 1901 was the worst month, with a recorded 2 831 black deaths. This represented a mortality rate of 372 per 1 000 per year, exceeding the highest figure for white deaths recorded in October 1901 at 344 per 1 000 per year. As was the case with the whites, the majority of black deaths (81 per cent) were children's. Though official figures are undoubtedly incomplete, they indicate that at least 14 154 blacks died in the concentration camps,[42] against a white figure of 27 927.

The great majority of black mortalities were caused by chicken pox, measles and dysentery, and may clearly be ascribed to the appalling conditions in the overcrowded camps. The huts and tents, often rigged up out of grain sacks, were not only too close to each other but were hopelessly inadequate at affording protection against wind and weather. Water, often scarce, was at times also polluted, and there was a shortage of firewood. Rations in the black camps were both poorer and smaller than those issued in white camps, since most blacks were forced to be self-supporting. Medical facilities were also inadequate.

Early in 1902 conditions in the black camps were improved, with particular attention being paid to raising the standard of food supplies. Cows were provided to ensure a supply of fresh milk and the scope of free rations was extended to include commodities like tinned milk and cornflour. Although the improvements resulted in a considerable drop in the mortality rate,

Camps for blacks were established alongside white concentration camps, and later close to the railway lines, providing the British with a ready supply of labour for menial tasks and for cultivating crops

Above left, & below Blacks loading wagons with their possessions en route to a concentration camp, while others wait patiently for the train that will transport them (*After Pretoria*)

Above right Mealie meal rations dispensed to blacks at Klerksdorp concentration camp in the Transvaal (*After Pretoria*)

Mortality in the black camps was high, particularly in late 1901-1902. A total of over 14 000 deaths was recorded. Improvements made to the white camps were not as swiftly extended to the black camps. Emily Hobhouse wrote in a letter, 'Is it generally known and realised at home that there are many large Native (coloured) camps dotted about? In my opinion these need looking into badly.' In this case her voice went unheeded

Above Armed black levies assist British troops clearing Brandwater Basin in 1901, to capture burghers (By courtesy of the National Army Museum, London)

Below Refugees in a 'white man's war' (*After Pretoria*)

they came too late. The concentration camps, both black and white, remain a tragic page in the history of the war.

Peace negotiations were already in progress between Milner and Kitchener and the Boer governments when the most serious of the confrontations between armed blacks and Boers occurred on the night of 5 May 1902 at Holkrantz, some 20 km north of Vryheid in the then southeastern Transvaal.

The Qulusi, a minor Zulu tribe whose territory had been expropriated by whites, claimed that the Boers were commandeering their horses and cattle without issuing receipts. Boer commandos had executed several tribesmen without trial, merely on suspicion that they had spied for the British. The Boers, on the other hand, claimed that the Qulusi had been passing information to the British and had attacked isolated burghers. Botha consequently ordered that all black women whose husbands were on armed service in the British army should be brought to Vryheid, their livestock confiscated and their huts burned down.

With the local British magistrate, A. J. Shepstone, apparently turning a blind eye knowingly, a Qulusi impi launched an attack on the Vryheid commando at Holkrantz. Qulusi rifles and assegais killed 56 burghers, including Field-Cornet J. Potgieter, who is reputed to have suffered no less than 45 stab wounds. Qulusi losses were 52 dead and 48 wounded.

The Holkrantz incident, happening so shortly before the Boer delegates met at Vereeniging on 15 May 1902, was a grim reminder to the Boers of the increasingly important role armed blacks were playing in the war. Botha and various other Vereeniging delegates emphasised the threat armed blacks posed both to the commandos and to the Boer women and children in the veld. Several delegates insisted that if Zulu hostility were to force them to vacate the southeastern Transvaal, the entire strategy of the guerrilla war would be placed in jeopardy. The commandos would be forced to operate within a smaller area, greatly increasing the danger of their being trapped against the blockhouse lines.

There is therefore no doubt that black resistance to the Boer forces and armed black collaboration with the British army had an important influence on the delegates' decision to sue for peace at Vereeniging. As Donald Denoon has recently said, 'Factors in the black–white dimension intruded upon the white–white dimension.' However, the effect of black participation in the war should be seen in perspective alongside such factors as the plight of the Boer women and children in the concentration camps, the physical devastation of the two Boer republics and the resulting shortage of food, and the unequal nature of the Boers' struggle against an overwhelming British majority.

CHAPTER 9

Attitudes in Europe and the USA

The war in South Africa provoked enormous interest in both Europe and the United States of America. Nevertheless, the European balance of power and in particular her supremacy at sea enabled Britain to conduct her struggle with the Boer republics without fear of foreign intervention.

Mutual distrust between the various European states meant that each attempted to provoke others into open support of the Boer republics, with the intention of emerging as the saviour of the British Empire if things went wrong. Though Europe was prepared to exploit Britain's position to its own advantage, no state wished to commit itself too far.

When the Netherlands and Russia neglected to invite the ZAR to the first Peace Conference in the Hague in May 1899 for fear of British disapproval, it was already clear that the European nations were not prepared to take active sides with the Boer republics against Britain.

What was the attitude of Germany, at the time the most powerful state on the European continent? Britain had already begun to foresee that her policy of 'splendid isolation' from Europe's affairs would be to her future disadvantage. Germany's abandonment of the Boer cause dates from the

Der Moloch verlangt neues Futter — ein Opfer sträubt sich noch!

A German view of British imperialism. Roberts and Chamberlain sacrifice their victims to Moloch; Rhodes stokes the fire (Postcard, Greenwall collection)

83

Kruger's European exile proved a saddening experience. A weary old man (*above*), he emerges from his lodgings at Hilversum in the Netherlands for his daily outing (*L'Illustration*, June 1901)

Below Germany in vain urges the Kaiser to receive the South African 'freedom hero'. Cartoon by Dutch artist Braakensiek (Greenwall collection)

moment British overtures to German statesmen were favourably received, as witnessed by the agreement of 30 August 1898 regarding Portugal.

Evidence that Kaiser Wilhelm II and the German government were well disposed towards Britain was a powerful deterrent to European nations considering intervening on behalf of the Boers. The fact that Germany had only begun to expand her fleet in earnest in 1897 and could not yet challenge British maritime supremacy, was probably the principal reason why the Boer republics could not expect Germany to save them. For the Boers it was unfortunate that the war occurred at the particular period when Britain was seeking rapprochement with Germany. By the end of the war the estrangement between these two great powers was already visible.

The Fashoda crisis of 1898 cost France a great deal of prestige with respect to Britain. Nevertheless Britain's friendship remained indispensable to France, in order to ensure the isolation of her arch-enemy Germany and regain Alsace-Lorraine, which she had lost to Germany in the Franco-Prussian War of 1871.

Russia alone among the European powers displayed sympathy with the Boer cause in government circles. E. Kandyba-Foxcroft has pointed out that Tsar Nicholas II cherished a deep-rooted hatred of Britain. However, Russia needed peace, in order to raise her economic and cultural levels. At the time of the Anglo-Boer War she was experiencing serious financial, industrial and agricultural crises and these prevented her from exploiting Britain's dilemma to either her own or the Boers' advantage. [43]

The USA's official attitude should be seen in the light of the 'Anglo-American understanding', a relationship that had only shortly before been strengthened by the Spanish-American War of 1898 after a period of coolness which had lasted all through the 19th century. The anglophile US Secretary of State, John Hay, was in particular responsible for the USA's official pro-British attitude during the Anglo-Boer War.

In the Netherlands many of the individual government members, as well as the young Queen Wilhelmina herself, were warmly sympathetic towards their kinsmen in the Boer republics. However, the Netherlands had become a minor power and was dependent on British protection for her overseas trade, particularly in the East. She therefore officially decided to adopt an expedient policy of neutrality in the Anglo-Boer War.

As for Portugal, a mere three days after the outbreak of the Anglo-Boer War she concluded a secret agreement with Britain whereby the British government promised to protect all Portuguese territories against her enemies. In exchange the Portuguese undertook to forbid the importation of munitions into the ZAR via Portuguese East Africa (Moçambique) for the duration of the war, in effect severing the Boer republics' only link with the outside world.

Within this diplomatic web, Dr W. J.

Leyds as minister plenipotentiary for the ZAR in Europe and Dr H. P. N. Muller, Consul General of the Free State in the Netherlands, had to plead the cause of the Boer republics. Leyds' task in Brussels was to sound out the European governments about the situation and to keep his own government informed, a task complicated by difficulties of communication and the fact that Europe and a Boer government, particularly one in the field, were not only physically but spiritually miles apart.

On 5 March 1900 Presidents Kruger and Steyn sent a cable to the British Prime Minister Lord Salisbury, stating that they were fighting to retain the indisputable independence of both republics as sovereign international states. On 9 and 11 March this was followed by requests to various powers to intervene in order to prevent further bloodshed.

Before these various governments could react, Salisbury replied that Britain was not prepared to agree to the independence of either the ZAR or the Free State. Immediately all hope of intervention by other powers was quashed, giving the governments concerned the opportunity to refuse Kruger and Steyn.

Meanwhile the two Boer presidents decided to send overseas a deputation consisting of A. Fischer, C. H. Wessels and A. D. W. Wolmarans, with the aim of obtaining foreign intervention or aid in restoring peace in South Africa, and also maintaining the independence of the two republics – a somewhat naïve quest.

The deputation arrived in Europe in April 1900. As G. D. Scholtz puts it, the deputation met more closed doors than open ones and heard more refusals than encouragement from statesmen. Despite enthusiasm reflected in general public opinion and the press, the Boer delegation drew one blank after the other, in the Netherlands, the USA, France, Germany and Russia. Queen Wilhelmina granted an audience, but the international position of the Netherlands precluded the rendering of any real assistance to the deputation.

In the USA the deputation made the tactical error of flirting with the opposition Democratic Party on the eve of the presidential election. Both Secretary of State John Hay and President McKinley assured the delegates of their sympathy for the bloody war in South Africa, but reminded them that US policy rested on impartial neutrality. This was not altogether true, just as the Netherlands government periodically displayed pro-Boer sentiments within the framework of its stated neutrality.

The deputation's visit to Europe was particularly ill-timed. Events in the East, including the Boxer Rebellion in China, were already pushing the war in South Africa into the background. In France President Loubet and the Minister of Foreign Affairs, Delcassé, provided the deputation with their third refusal, since the French were not prepared to risk 85 years of peace with Britain by taking up the Boer cause.

The German Kaiser made certain that he was unable to receive the deputation in Berlin. They then proceeded to the Russian capital, St Petersburg, where the Tsar also refused to receive them, although he granted Leyds an audience. According to Leyds the Tsar indicated willingness to intervene on behalf of the republics provided assurance were obtained from the German Kaiser that Germany would not side with Britain. The Tsar expressed a sympathy with the Boer cause which in all likelihood stemmed largely from anti-British sentiments.

The Boer deputation had failed in its mission. Until the end of the war its members remained chiefly in the Netherlands, witnesses to a gradual waning of interest in the South African struggle.

When the Boer republics decided on 28 August 1900 to send the widely respected President Kruger to Europe, they were consciously playing their last card. In an open expression of sympathy which probably cannot be regarded as a violation of neutrality, Queen Wilhelmina placed the Dutch warship *Gelderland* at Kruger's disposal to bring him to Europe from Lourenço Marques (Maputo). The aged President landed in Marseilles on 22 November 1900. As G. D. Scholtz has said, this was Kruger's last journey to plead for the republican cause.[45]

Up to this stage the deputation had basically aimed at securing intervention by one or more of the great powers, in the expectation of diplomatic mediation to end the war and at the same time persuading Britain to recognise the complete independence of both republics. Now for the first time Kruger spoke of arbitration, with an impartial head of state to decide whether the republics would retain their independence. Kruger's personal viewpoint was fundamentally naïve. He regarded the republics' cause as a just and therefore holy one, on behalf of which the great powers were duty bound to intervene – so completely was he out of touch with world politics.

Kruger's meetings with Loubet and Delcassé in France were fruitless, as might have been foreseen by anyone in touch with contemporary political trends. But it was the German Kaiser's refusal even to receive Kruger that swept away the very foundations of the president's mission. The interest shown by European statesmen in the war in South Africa faded dramatically. The only path left to Kruger and the deputation, as well as Muller in the Netherlands and Leyds in Brussels, was to stir public sympathy for the Boer cause in Europe to the pitch where it might possibly compel the various governments to action.

Press and public sympathy in Europe had been steadily growing for the Boers since the Jameson Raid, particularly after the outbreak of the Anglo-Boer War. The press played a major role in shaping public opinion, with most European newspapers venting their anti-British feelings in a vehement defence of the Boer cause, supporting individuals and organisations everywhere who wanted to help the republics. Funds were launched to relieve the Boer plight and ambulance teams were assembled and equipped, especially in the Netherlands, Germany and Russia, and sent to the South African front.

Unparalleled enthusiasm for the Boer cause followed their brilliant victories in the field in December 1899. When the tide of the war turned after February 1900 and the Boers began to suffer successive reverses, some supporters abroad lost interest in the war. However, the majority merely intensified their disapproval of Britain as the 'oppressor of nations'. The arrival of the Boer deputation, and later of Kruger, kept enthusiasm for the Boer cause high.

Sympathy for the Boers was strongest in the Netherlands. Unlike other European nations, where divergent groups still supported the British cause, the Dutch were pro-Boer to a man. In Africa their kinsmen were pointing the way to a return of the golden age for the Netherlands. In Belgium both the Flemish and the Walloons widely supported the Boer cause – the Flemish because they joined the Dutch in the organisation, the Algemene Nederlandse Verbond, in identifying with the Boer nation, and the Walloons because they shared with France not only their language but a mutual hatred of Great Britain. No patriotic Frenchman had forgotten the diplomatic defeat France had suffered at the hands of Britain, its colonial competitor, at Fashoda in 1898.

Like the French, the Russians in the first place were anti-British and therefore pro-Boer; any setback for Britain was regarded as a victory. The Russian nation revealed great admiration for the handful of Boers who, like the knights of past times, had dared to challenge their mighty common enemy. Rural Russians in particular identified with the simple, God-fearing Boers whose intense love of the land they could so well understand.

The pro-Boer enthusiasm of the German people also developed naturally from deepening anti-British sentiments. In German eyes Afrikaners belonged to the same ethnic group, and they took pride in Boer achievements.

The USA was the scene of an extensive pro-Boer propaganda campaign. In the Midwest, where large numbers of German and Dutch immigrants had settled, as well as in Irish circles, sympathy for the Boer cause was overwhelming. In the Anglo-Saxon areas of the USA pro-British sentiment tended to triumph, despite a measure of sympathy for the Boers – Americans could recall their own War of Independence against Britain in 1776-83. Yet the Boer deputation, and American helpers such as Montagu White, were unable to make more than a superficial impression on the changeable sentiments of the general public. American worship of success and their sympathy for the underdog brought the Boers much admiration, but when their early victories faded, and the great battles did not follow each other in quick succession, American interest swung elsewhere.

As has been mentioned, the end of the Anglo-Boer War was signalled by the note sent by Netherlands Prime Minister Kuyper to the British government on 25 January 1902. Europe was on the whole relieved by the peace: though Britain could not be prevented from depriving the Boer republics of their independence, the major issue of contention towards the end of the war – the terrible suffering on the South African veld – was over.

After the conclusion of peace Generals de Wet, Botha and de la Rey travelled to England, the Netherlands, Belgium, France and Germany to raise funds for the indigent Boer women and children. On the Continent they were particularly well received, yet the results of their fundraising campaign were disappointing. Europe had her own problems to consider.

Christiaan de Wet was widely regarded as the greatest Boer hero of the war for his almost miraculous evasion of the British army. In this reverential French cartoon, he carries 'the hope of the last rebels' with him (*L'Assiette au Beurre*)

L'INSAISISSABLE DEWET

... Seul un misérable fou refuse jusqu'ici de se rendre. C'est lui qui porte l'ESPÉRANCE des derniers rebelles.

CHAPTER 10

The aftermath

The Treaty of Vereeniging established British supremacy in South Africa – for the first time since the Great Trek the entire country was part of the British Empire.

As High Commissioner for South Africa and Governor of the Orange River Colony and the Transvaal (as the two former Boer republics were now known), Lord Alfred Milner's most urgent task was to repair war damage in the new colonies. For this monumental task he enlisted the cooperation of a group of able young men like Lionel Curtis, Patrick Duncan and Richard Feetham, who were soon dubbed 'Milner's kindergarten'.

The repatriation and resettlement of displaced inhabitants from the former Boer republics took priority. Large numbers of Boer prisoners of war, many of them abroad, plus the Boer civilians and blacks in the concentration camps, the bitter enders, joiners and Uitlanders, all had to be resettled in devastated regions where 30 000 homesteads had been burned down and farms had been stripped of livestock and crops. Separate repatriation councils were instituted for joiners.

In terms of the Treaty of Vereeniging the British government made £3

Left A hero's welcome for the City Imperial Volunteers, returning to London in 1900. The return of British regiments after peace was far less spectacular. Drawing by Melton Prior (Greenwall collection)

Opposite One of the last commandos leaves the field. Sjambok in hand, Fouché rides into Cradock under escort (*After Pretoria*)

million, plus interest-free loans to nearly the same extent, available to the Boers to cover the total resettlement programme and provide basic commodities for those worst affected by the war damage. Landowners were to be provided with implements and seeds to enable them to rebuild their farms. An additional sum of £2 million was allocated as compensation to British subjects, neutral foreign subjects and blacks. The total cost of the repatriation and resettlement programme amounted to some £16½ million. The programme was on the whole successful, although naturally no group was really satisfied with its share.

An urgent goal of the British reconstruction in South Africa was to restore and then improve pre-war levels of production in the goldmining industry. Britain envisaged establishing a modernised state that could keep pace with the requirements of a growing mining industry. South African gold production increased from just over £12 600 000 in 1903 to £27 500 000 in 1907, a material recovery that proved an essential prelude to the movement towards union. Much of the credit goes to Milner, although his importation of indentured Chinese labourers for the goldmines evoked sharp criticism from the Liberal Party which came into power in Britain after the war, and caused division in British circles in the Transvaal. It was also one of the spurs to political reorganisation among Afrikaners.

The devastation wrought by the British scorched earth policy, as well as a series of droughts in the immediate post-war years, had a profound socio-economic effect on the Afrikaner. Before the war there had been relatively few burghers in the Free State who had not shared in the prosperity of the republic, although in the ZAR white poverty had been on the increase. In the immediate post-war years, however, the poor white problem in both colonies gained alarming proportions. Landowners sank into poverty and were unable to offer landless families (bywoners) a home – particularly those who had been joiners and hensoppers during the war.

Although some bywoners and collaborators were accommodated in specially created settlements in the eastern and western Transvaal, thousands of poor whites flocked to the cities to be absorbed into the labour market of the mines and industries. The social disintegration was widespread. Nevertheless, South Africa's development into a modern state with a sound inflow of capital was to enable a younger generation of Afrikaners to seize political leadership. Most of them were ambitious farmers who were more receptive to capitalistic enterprises than their predecessors.

For black South Africans, the war had brought only confusion and calamity. A shortage of basic implements and seed delayed the economic recovery of those blacks resettled from the concentration camps. In the Transvaal the Repatriation Department for instance spent £1 183 594 on the rehabilitation of white agriculture, against the £16 194 received by the Native Refugee Department towards black recovery. Once again, the scorched earth policy had exacerbated wide-spread poverty, and in several eastern Transvaal districts black communities were still on the brink of famine six months after the war. The droughts of 1902 and 1903 worsened the situation. Many black peasants were forced to become wage earners employed by whites. Only those peasants whose districts had been relatively untouched by the war made economic progress afterwards.

The post-war period was a time of great disillusionment for blacks in South Africa. Contrary to expectation, their working conditions did not improve. Black mine wages were lowered, controls over black labourers were strengthened and conditions in the mining compounds deteriorated.

The chiefs whose tribes had served the British during the war found that they received very little in return. Lentshwe, the Kgatla chief who had kept the Boers out of large areas of the western Transvaal, waited in vain for an extension of the Kgatla reserve which would unite his people in the Bechuanaland Protectorate with those in the Transvaal. Sekhukhune II cherished hopes of receiving a larger territory for the Pedi, as well as greater control over Pedi affairs; neither was forthcoming. Zulu co-operation with the British was rewarded by the opening up of large tracts of Zululand to white settlement.

According to Warwick, perhaps the most disappointed were the black elite, who had pinned high hopes of political advancement on a British victory. Instead, the peace treaty postponed the question of the vote for blacks, coloureds and Indians in both new colonies until self-government should be granted. Black leaders soon realised that a change of government in the former republics would not ensure the extension of Cape franchise qualifications to the Transvaal and Orange River Colony. The discriminatory laws of the ZAR and the Free State were not only largely retained by the Milner administration, but in some cases were even widened in scope. The Peace of Vereeniging had ensured that, for all practical purposes, political power would remain in the hands of white South Africa.

The war had far-reaching effects on the white political structure. Milner's desire to turn South Africa into a useful link in the British imperial chain was expressed in a policy of anglicisation and denationalisation of the Afrikaner. Until these strategies strengthened by British immigration, had firmly established British influence in the former republics, he intended both to remain crown colonies. Until such time, no federation of South African states would be allowed to emerge as a self-governing British dominion.

Milner's task seemed an easy one. Afrikaners had emerged from the war deeply divided: British loyalists, Cape rebels, bitter enders, hensoppers and joiners all represented separate groups. Bitter enders in particular made no secret of their disgust and hatred for collaborators with the British. Boers judged as disloyal became outcasts from Afrikaner society and even from Afrikaner churches. A separate Scout Church with seven parishes was established in 1903, but half-hearted support by the National Scouts and the colonial government led to its disappearance by 1906.

Through a policy of reconciliation, Louis Botha was largely successful in healing the breach in Afrikaner ranks. Mutual discontent among bitter enders and collaborators alike concerning inadequate financial compensation by the British government, as well as the

public pleas for forgiveness voiced by many joiners, gave Botha's policy weight.

Boer resistance to British supremacy, and the sacrifices and suffering of the war years, were deeply engraved in Afrikaner memory. The war, like Milner's anglicisation policy after it, stimulated a revival of Afrikaner nationalism. Although peace had left the Afrikaner without political power, his immediate reaction to 'Milnerism' emerged in the form of a cultural revival: the Tweede Taalbeweging. This second language movement, an attempt both to establish and develop Afrikaans, was a direct manifestation of the Afrikaner's struggle to retain his identity. The poetry of Eugène Marais, Louis Leipoldt, Totius and Jan Celliers, demonstrating that Afrikaans was a subtle language capable of expressing profound ideas, served to strengthen the political consciousness of the Afrikaner, who came to regard the 19th century as the Eeuw van Onrecht – the Century of Wrong. Vereeniging had not, as Milner had intended, signalled the end of the Afrikaner nation but rather its vigorous revival.

Among the political parties that emerged after the war was the Het Volk Party founded in 1905 by the Transvaal Afrikaners under the leadership of men like Louis Botha, Schalk Burger, Koos de la Rey and Jan Smuts. In the Free State the Orangia Unie was formed in 1906 with Barry Hertzog, Abraham Fischer and Christiaan de Wet as leaders. In 1903 the old Afrikaner Bond of the Cape became the South African Party.

Sir Henry Campbell-Bannerman's Liberal Party won the British election in 1905. The victory had two important results for South Africa. Firstly, Milner vanished from the South African political scene, although his followers such as Lionel Curtis and Patrick Duncan continued to uphold British imperialism in the country. Secondly, in December 1906 the Liberal government in Britain granted responsible government to the Transvaal, with the Orange River Colony following in June 1907. In the general elections of 1907, the Het Volk Party and its English-speaking allies defeated the divided opposition, and Louis Botha became Prime Minister

of the Transvaal. In the Orange River Colony the Orangia Unie triumphed, with Abraham Fischer becoming Prime Minister.

After Vereeniging, some 10 500 Cape rebels who had fought with the republican Boers during the war lost the right to vote for a period of five years, a factor contributing largely to the victory of Dr Jameson's Progressive Party in the Cape Colony in 1904.

By 1907 all four South African colonies shared the same constitutional status, intensifying the desire for unification among colonial British imperialists as well as among Afrikaners. The victory of John X. Merriman's South African Party in the Cape general election of 1908 meant, in effect, that a mere six years after the war Afrikaners were in power in three out of the four South African colonies. Imperialism had lost the initiative in South Africa, and men like Smuts, Merriman, M. T. Steyn and Hertzog took the lead. After the National Convention, the Union of South Africa was born on 31 May 1910 under the British flag.

The Anglo-Boer War of 1899-1902 left a near indelible impression on the Afrikaner. Economically, politically and personally he had lost so much that even Botha and Smuts' rapprochement with the former enemy was unable to prevent the Afrikaner's lasting alienation from Britain – and from British imperialism in particular. With the 1914 Rebellion during the First World War and again during the Second World War, these feelings came to the fore. The republican ideal lived on, so that the establishment of the Republic of South Africa on 31st May 1961 marked the final erasure of the political significance of the Peace of Vereeniging.

Top left The Boers returned to the rural life that is celebrated on this Dutch postcard sold to aid women and children from the concentration camps

Left centre Chamberlain succeeded in painting the Transvaal and Free State red, as the coloured map (*below*) of the British Empire after the war proudly confirms

Top right King Edward's peace message urged his South African subjects to co-operate in their new 'common country'

Bottom Lord Roberts' heroic image remained unsullied; blame for the darkest aspects of the war fell on Kitchener (Greenwall collection)

Uitgegeven door de Haagsche Pro-Boervereeniging te 's Gravenhage, Molenstraat 4, ten bate van de gevangen Boerenvrouwen en -kinderen in Z.A.

DIE MIELIEPIT.

Die mielieplant is door Gods hand
    Aan ons Transvaal gegeven,
Dat mensch en dier nog altijd hier,
    Kan eten en kan leven.

Ons arme land is zwart gebrand
    Door d' Engelsche gebroedsel.
Maar die mieliekop raak nog nie op,
    Hij schenk ons drank en voedsel.

God zij gedank, nie die soort drank,
    Wat door ou Marks 1) gestook wordt.
Maar mieliemat die drink ons, wat
    In die koffiepot gekook wordt.

Vrijstaat het 2) brood. Ons bondgenoot
    Wensch ons geluk daarmede.
Maar voor ons deel — met mieliemeel
    Is ons al hoog tevrede.

In' vredestijd — dan zonder strijd —
    Het 2) korenmeel meer waarde.
Maar met oorlog is mielies tog
    Die beste kos op aarde.

Maak kooigoed 3) van zijn blare dan,
    Zijn stroak kan vuur en pijp maak,
Zelfs met zijn as kan jij kleere wasch.
    As jij hem eerst tot zeep maak.

Of wil die Boer ook groene voer
    Aan perd of schaap of os ge' —
Dan weet hij goed wat hij doen moet,
    Wil hij hem lekker kos ge'. —

Maar die mieliepit, as hij is dit
    Waarvoor ons God het meest moet loven,
Met hom en vlijs 4) zal ons Khaki wijs,
    Ons voik die blijf nog boven.

Op hoeveel wijs tot lekker spijs,
    Jij mielies klaar kan krijge,
Is ho' mijn gal en daarom zal
    Ik dit nu maar verzwijge.

Maar geef mij 'n hap van mieliepap,
    Dan zal ik niks meer zoeke,
Want glo 5) mij vrij, dit smaak vir mij,
    Nog lekkerder dan koeke.

Transvaal bezit die mieliepit;
    Laat Khaki ruk en piukke.
Zijn twak is nat 6); ons land te vat
    Zal hem zoo nooit gelukke.

Waarom is daar een adelaar
    Op ons Transvaalsche wapen ?
Zet eers daarop een mieliekop
    En laat die roofvo'el schrape.

                          F. W. REITZ.

1) Samuel Marks: Whisky v Hatherly distillery. 2) Heeft. 3) Matrasvulsel, 4) Vleesch.
5) Geloof. 6) „Zijn tabak is nat": hetgeen beteekent „zijn kracht is gedaan"

Raphael Tuck & Sons' Peace Souvenir Post Card, No. 662.

PEACE!

Lord Kitchener to Secretary of State for War.

PRETORIA, May 31 (11.15 p.m).

Negotiations with Boer delegates.

The document containing terms of surrender was signed here this evening, at 10.30 p.m. by all Boer representatives as well as by Lord Milner and myself.

BUCKINGHAM PALACE, June 1st, 1902.

"The King has received the welcome news of the cessation of hostilities in South Africa with infinite satisfaction, and trusts that peace may be speedily followed by the restoration of prosperity in his new dominions, and that the feelings necessarily engendered by war will give place to the earnest co-operation of all his Majesty's South African subjects in promoting the welfare of their common country."

"GRACED WITH WREATHS OF VICTORY."
Shakespeare.

Copied from the original painting by B. Faustin, Esq., by kind permission of the Proprietors of the "Ludgate Magazine."

Raphael Tuck & Sons "Empire Postcard No. 1588.

"A HUNDRED THOUSAND WELCOMES!"
Shakespeare

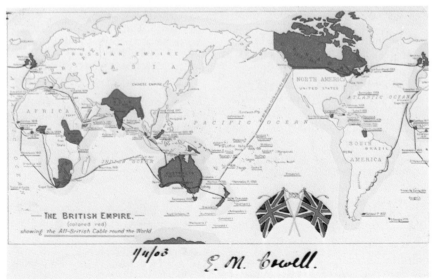

— THE BRITISH EMPIRE, —
(colored red)
showing the All-British Cable round the World

References

1 Quoted by W. Nasson: 'Tommy Atkins in South Africa' (In P. Warwick (ed): *The South African War*, p 134)
2 Quoted by E. J. Hardy: *Mr Thomas Atkins*, pp 304 & 294
3 Quoted by J. Meintjes: *De la Rey – Lion of the West*, p 215
4 Quoted by J. H. Breytenbach: *Die geskiedenis van die Tweede Vryheidsoorlog in Suid-Afrika, 1899-1902*, I, p 140 (translation)
5 J. J. Oberholster (ed): *Dagboek van Oskar Hintrager* (In *Christiaan de Wet-Annale 2*, p 60); S. Izedinova: *A few months with the Boers*, p 67
6 W. H. Ackermann: *Opsaal: herinneringe aan die Tweede Vryheidsoorlog*, p 290; A. J. V. Burger: *Worsteljare*, p 84
7 C. R. de Wet: *Three years' war*, p 81
8 C. R. de Wet: *Three years' war*, p 14
9 J. J. Oberholster (ed): *Dagboek van Oskar Hintrager* (In *Christiaan de Wet-Annale 2*, p 141)
10 B. J. Viljoen: *My reminiscences of the Anglo-Boer War*, p 156
11 H. Ver Loren van Themaat: *Twee jaren in den Boerenoorlog*, p 87
12 A. G. Hales: *Campaign pictures of the war in South Africa (1899-1900)*, p 102; R. H. Davis: *With both armies in South Africa*, pp 93, 192
13 A. G. Oberholster (ed): *Oorlogsdagboek van Jan F. E. Celliers*, 2.11.1899, p 20, & 10.10.1900, p 146 (translation)
14 A. G. Oberholster (ed): *Oorlogsdagboek van Jan F. E. Celliers*, 30.12.1899, p 51 & 11.12.1900, p 178 (translation)
15 A. G. Oberholster (ed): *Oorlogsdagboek van Jan F. E. Celliers*, 19.4.1902, p 368 (translation)
16 Quoted by S. P. R. Oosthuizen: *Die beheer, behandeling en lewe van die krygsgevangenes gedurende die Anglo-Boereoorlog, 1899-1902*, pp 160, 566-567
17 Quoted by S. P. R. Oosthuizen: *Die beheer, behandeling en lewe van die krygsgevangenes gedurende die Anglo-Boereoorlog, 1899-1902*, p 338 (translation)
18 S. P. R. Oosthuizen: *Die beheer, behandeling en lewe van die krygsgevangenes gedurende die Anglo-Boereoorlog, 1899-1902*, p 573
19 Quoted by S. B. Spies: *Methods of barbarism?* p 125
20 S. B. Spies: *Methods of barbarism?* p 118
21 S. B. Spies: *Methods of barbarism?* pp 185-191

22 L. M. Phillipps: *With Rimington*, p 202
23 *Stemme uit die vrouekampe*, statement by Mrs B. Breytenbach, p 73
24 E. Neethling: *Mag ons vergeet?* Statement by Miss M. Els, p 34
25 S. B. Spies: *Methods of barbarism?* p 215
26 A. C. Martin: *The concentration camps 1900-1902*, p 31
27 S. B. Spies: *Methods of barbarism?* p 269
28 A. G. Oberholster (ed): *Oorlogsdagboek van Jan F. E. Celliers*, 2.11.1901, p 310, & 27.5.1902, p 380
29 A. G. Oberholster (ed): *Oorlogsdagboek van Jan F. E. Celliers*, 27.5.1902, p 380
30 E. Neethling: *Mag ons vergeet?* Statement by A. S. du Toit, p 78
31 B. J. Viljoen: *Mijne herinneringen uit den Anglo-Boeren-Oorlog*, pp 242-243 (translation)
32 E. Neethling: *Mag ons vergeet?* Statement by Mrs M. Kriel, p 6
33 A. M. Grundlingh: *Die 'Hendsoppers' en 'Joiners'*, pp 23-25; A. M. Grundlingh: 'Collaborators in Boer society' (In P. Warwick (ed): *The South African War*, p 261)
34 A. M. Grundlingh: 'Collaborators in Boer society' (In P. Warwick, (ed), *The South African War*, p 261)
35 Transvaal Archives, Leyds-archives 781(1): VII, report by Captain Ram and Lieutenant Thomson, p 28
36 P. Warwick: *Black people and the South African War 1899-1902*, pp 24-25
37 O. J. O. Ferreira (ed): *Memoirs of General Ben Bouwer*, p 51
38 W. H. Ackermann: *Opsaal: herinneringe aan die Tweede Vryheidsoorlog*, p 367
39 W. H. Ackermann: *Opsaal: herinneringe aan die Tweede Vryheidsoorlog*, p 369
40 S. B. Spies: *Methods of barbarism?* p 227
41 S. B. Spies: *Methods of barbarism?* p 230; P. Warwick: *Black people and the South African War 1899-1902*, pp 51-152
42 P. Warwick: *Black people and the South African War 1899-1902*, pp 151-152
43 E. Kandyba-Foxcroft: *Russia and the Anglo-Boer War 1899-1902*, chapters 1 & 2
44 G. D. Scholtz: *Europa en die Tweede Vryheidsoorlog*, p 98
45 G. D. Scholtz: *Europa en die Tweede Vryheidsoorlog*, p 115

Acknowledgements

The illustration of this book has been largely made possible by the generosity of Ryno Greenwall, who permitted us access to his remarkable collection of drawings and paintings, postcards, periodicals, books and objects associated with the Anglo-Boer War. We would like to thank him and his wife Yvonne for their patience and help.

Thanks also go to the following people and institutions for their advice and help with pictorial research: the Cape Archives; Dr Christo Grobbelaar; the Institute for Cartographic Analysis at Stellenbosch University; the National Army Museum, London; the South African Library, Cape Town; and Elrethe van Rooyen for the maps on pp 12, 32 and 56.

Permission to reproduce Guy Butler's translation of Jan Celliers' poem 'Dis Al' on p 53 was kindly granted by Oxford University Press Southern Africa.

The title page illustration is a watercolour of the Royal Horse Artillery in action, by 'J.A.H.C.', from the Greenwall collection. The half-title page shows 'A Boer father and son ready for the front', from Cassell's *History of the Boer War* (Volume I).

Illustrations have also been drawn from the following books in the Greenwall collection and the South African Library (titles have occasionally been abbreviated in the captions):
After Pretoria: the Guerilla war, by H. W. Wilson (1902); *The Anglo-Boer War 1899-1900*, by Dennis Edwards (1901); *British Commanders in the Transvaal* (1900); *Buller's Campaign with Natal Field Force of 1900*, by E. B. Knox (1902); *Die Buren und der Südafrikanische Krieg* (1902); *Heroes of the Boer War* by F. Rompel (1903); *Khaki in South Africa* (1900); *Onze Krijgs-officieren* (1904); *South Africa and the Transvaal War*, by L. Creswicke (1900-03); *De Vrijheids-Oorlog van de Boeren in Zuid-Afrika* (1900); *War Impressions*, by Mortimer Menpes (1901); *War Pictures* (1900); *War with the Boers*, by H. Brown & E. Grew (1900-02); *With the Flag to Pretoria*, by H. W. Wilson (1900-01).

Bibliography

Amery, L. S. (ed): *The Times history of the war in South Africa.* 7v. London, 1900-1909

Barnard, C. J.: *Generaal Louis Botha op die Natalse front, 1899-1900.* Cape Town, 1970

Breytenbach, J. H. (ed): *Gedenkalbum van die Tweede Vryheidsoorlog.* Cape Town, 1949

Breytenbach, J. H.: *Die geskiedenis van die Tweede Vryheidsoorlog in Suid-Afrika, 1899-1902.* 4v. Pretoria, 1969-1977

Comaroff, J. L. (ed): *The Boer War diary of Sol T. Plaatje: an African at Mafeking.* Johannesburg, 1973

Davis, R. H.: *With both armies in South Africa.* New York, 1900

De Wet, C. R.: *De Strijd tusschen Boer en Brit.* Amsterdam, 1902

De Wet, C. R.: *Three years' war (October 1899-June 1902).* London, 1902

De Wet, C. R.: *Die stryd tussen Boer en Brit.* Cape Town, 1959

Doyle, A. C.: *The Great Boer War.* London, 1902

Grundlingh, A. M.: *Die 'Hendsoppers' en 'Joiners'. Die rasionaal en verskynsel van verraad.* Pretoria & Cape Town, 1979

Hardy, E. J.: *Mr Thomas Atkins.* London, 1900

Hillegas, H. C.: *With the Boer forces.* London, 1901

Hobhouse, E.: *The brunt of the war and where it fell.* London, 1902

Kestell, J. D.: *Met de Boeren-commando's.* Amsterdam, 1903

Kestell, J. D.: *Through shot and flame.* London, 1903

Kruger, R.: *Good-bye Dolly Gray: the story of the Boer War.* London, 1959

Marais, J. S.: *The fall of Kruger's republic.* Oxford, 1961

Maurice, F. M. and Grant, M. H.: *History of the war in South Africa, 1899-1902, compiled by direction of His Majesty's government.* 4v + 4v maps. London, 1906-1910

Neethling, E.: *Mag ons vergeet?* Cape Town, 1938

Oberholster, A. G. (ed): *Oorlogsdagboek van Jan F. E. Celliers, 1899-1902.* Pretoria, 1978

Oberholster, J. J. (ed): *Dagboek van Oskar Hintrager* (In: *Christiaan De Wet-Annale 2.* Bloemfontein, 1973)

Oosthuizen, S. P. R.: *Die beheer, behandeling en lewe van die Krygsgevangenes gedurende die Anglo-Boereoorlog, 1899-1902.* Bloemfontein, 1975

Pakenham, T.: *The Boer War.* London & Johannesburg, 1979

Pakenham, T.: *Die Boere-oorlog.* Johannesburg, 1981

Pretorius, F.: *Kommandolewe tydens die Anglo-Boereoorlog 1899-1902.* Cape Town, 1991.

Reitz. D.: *Commando: a Boer journal of the Boer War.* London, 1929

Scholtz, G. D.: *Europa en die Tweede Vryheidsoorlog, 1899-1902.* Johannesburg & Pretoria, 1939

Scholtz, G. D.: *Die oorsake van die Tweede Vryheidsoorlog.* 2v. Johannesburg, 1947

Scholtz, G. D.: *Die Tweede Vryheidsoorlog, 1899-1902.* Johannesburg, 1960

Scholtz, Leopold (ed): *Beroemde Suid-Afrikaanse krygsmanne.* Cape Town, 1984

Smith, I.R.: *The Origins of the South African War 1899-1902.* London, 1996.

Spies, S. B.: *Methods of barbarism? Roberts and Kitchener and civilians in the Boer Republics, January 1900-May 1902.* Cape Town & Pretoria, 1977

Stemme uit die vrouekampe. Gedurende die Tweede Vryheids Oorlog tussen Boer en Brit van 1899 tot 1902. Foreword: Potchefstroom, 1925

Viljoen, B. J.: *Mijne herinneringen uit den Anglo-Boeren-Oorlog.* Amsterdam, 1902

Viljoen, B. J.: *My reminiscences of the Anglo-Boer War.* London, 1902

Warwick, P.: *Black people and the South African War, 1899-1902.* Cambridge, 1983

Warwick, P. (ed): *The South African War. The Anglo-Boer War 1899-1902.* London, 1980

Index

Opposite Sergeant and Bugler, 1st Argyle and Sutherland Highlanders (*Transvaal War*)